To Where the Sun Sets

A Family History in Stories &
How to Find & Tell Your Own

Susan Hart Snyder

My stories come from my family's letters and diaries, photographs, and newspaper articles. They also come from the mouths of my parents and other relatives. As in the game of telephone that children play, much of my oral history has been passed from one person to the next over generations. That means the original story has very likely been altered by time. To make the stories come alive I insert comments and, on occasion, even entire conversations that never took place. As with oral tradition, it's story truth – not the six o'clock news reel.

Front Cover Photo: Maria & family from the "Callings" chapter. Left to right: Emma, August, August, Olga, Arthur, Maria, Martha.

Back Cover Photo: Eugene, Polly (on back of chair), & unknown cat from the "Golden State" chapter.

ISBN: 978-0-9974224-5-0

This book is dedicated to those family members who understood that someday, somehow, someone was going to want to sift through letters and photographs, trinkets and treasures to make real the lives represented by them. Thank you to Margaret, Harry B, Imogene, Lincoln, Link, Marie, Myrtle, Dixie, Ted, and the rest. You made time travel possible. That's my Aunt Myrtle by the gasoline sign on the corner, and my great-grandmother Camilla in the crosswalk. They are in downtown Los Angeles, probably coming from or going to the main library branch, where Myrtle did much of her genealogy research.

Photo taken in the early 1950s.

CONTENTS

So we beat on, boats against the current,

borne back ceaselessly into the past.

F. Scott Fitzgerald *The Great Gatsby*

INTRODUCTION
TELL A STORY – SAVE A LIFE

When I began writing my family history, I knew that it was about more than just getting the facts down. It was about recording my own stories as a gift to my family – yes – but, it was also about encouraging you to write yours. Not in the, *wouldn't it be nice if you interviewed Aunt Martha and passed on her tale about fighting off pythons in the Amazon jungle* sense. No. I mean in the *we are losing civilization as we know it and the only way we're going to save it is by communicating face to face* sense.

I mean it. It's a mission, folks.

A few months ago, my husband and I were having dinner at a local restaurant. We were seated on an outside patio between a multi-generation group and a family of four. The grandparents behind us were engaged in lively conversation with their grandchildren about their activities and school. They shared stories about recent events in their own lives and excitement with their daughter about the impending birth of the next grandchild.

That's right. I'm an unapologetic eavesdropper.

The family of four on the other side of us included the parents, a two year old and a five month old. The parents and two year old all had their faces buried in smartphones. The infant sat on his mother's lap staring at the table. No one coocooed at his cuteness. No one tried to make him smile. He was totally docile. Yes. The kids were being *good*. But that kind of *good* teaches nothing. Not how to interact with the world. Just how to be stumps.

There's a battle raging to free people from their glass box

prisons and engage them in reality – in the glory of nature; the healing presence of another; the value of the moment. Loss is unacceptable. But what can we do?

We can win the war by using every opportunity to interact with each other in our own unique ways.

In the introduction to the book *Outliers,* Malcom Gladwell tells the story of Italians who immigrated to Roseto, Pennsylvania. Researchers became interested in their much longer than average lifespans due to their lack of heart disease, ulcers, suicide, alcoholism, and drug addiction; and also in their low crime rate. The Roseto population cooked with lard and sugar. There wasn't anything unique about their genes. What could it be?

Community. Or, what my son likes to call, social capital.

Their doors were always open. Multi-generations lived in the same homes. They walked arm in arm. They shared their lives. They shared their stories.

As a teacher of American literature, I always ended the school year with a unit on the Vietnam War era. The accompanying assignment was for my students to interview someone from that time period and write his or her story. It could be a soldier, army nurse, anti-war protester, or Vietnamese boat person – anyone who had a tie to that volatile time.

Stumped for someone to interview, as she was driving one of our local freeways, one of my students noticed a motorcycle rider with *Hells Angels Vietnam Vet* embroidered across the back of his black leather jacket. She followed him down the exit ramp and then signaled for him to pull over. When she approached him about sharing his war story with her, he agreed. They sat down at a picnic bench in a nearby park and she got her interview.

After hearing my student's proud tale of the ingenuity and daring it took for her to find her interviewee, I figured it was only a matter of time before her parents darkened my classroom door. Why, they would demand, had I assigned their daughter the task of stalking motorcycle gang members! They fortunately never showed. And Hells Angels not withstanding, I still think it was one of the most meaningful assignments of my teaching career.

The stories my students recorded opened them to a world that had been locked away since the fall of Saigon. And in some cases unlocked mysteries about their own parents.

In one story, the sullen moods of a father were clarified by the revelation that he had borne the heavy burden of a life or death decision – one involving far more than his own life. While piloting a bomber on an outgoing run, still over South Vietnam, the engines started to sputter and die. That left him with only seconds to make a choice. One – crash and potentially kill himself and his crewmates. Or two – lighten the plane by dropping his payload of bombs on an area populated by locals to give the plane and crew a chance to make it back to the base. He lived to tell the tale. We know the consequence of his choice. It was one that would haunt him for the rest of his life.

Through the tale of a late-night knock at the door, another student learned of her mother's devastating encounter with the consequences of war. On the other side of that door were two rigid-backed soldiers bearing an official document. She need not read it. They need not speak. For she knew the minute she opened that door, she had become the latest in a long line of very young widows that stretched back through the course of U.S. military history. And the course of *her life* was forever changed.

Through those stories, those shared moments and memories, my students made deep connections to family, friends, and even strangers. Those stories gave voice to the past. They built bridges to the present that led them to a greater understanding of our world and each other.

That's the power of stories. That, and so much more.

Stories are instructive, inspirational, entertaining, and unifying.

Stories are truth derived from fact and imagination.

Stories are *magic*. They grant the teller the power to travel through time, resurrect the dead, and sketch their souls.

I exercised that power while writing my family history. Not by digging up the entire human family, mind you. Just my own. And in the telling, I wove threads of villains and heroes; visionaries and schemers; adventurers and artists into one vibrant imperfect tapestry, loose strands and all. Because, don't those loose strands make for some of the best stories?

Around our household, when we say, "What are we going to do with Charles?" it's with a smile at an inside joke about a multi-great-grandfather. Despite the two hundred plus years that separate us from Charles, we've grown to love the guy – because of, *not in spite of*, his status as official village ne'er-do-well. You'll find a part of his story in the "Villains and Black Sheep" chapter.

When you read my stories, you should know that our family doesn't subscribe to the "blood is thicker than water" maxim. We share little DNA with several of the folks in my stories. What we do share with them is a history so profound that it forges into family. Therefore, we don't label our step-relatives *step*, and we don't worry about whether you actually *are* or *are not* our fifth cousin twice removed. If you raised us, cared for us, or unconditionally loved us, warts and all, you're in. And, by the way, you can also make the cut if you're so dang colorful that you become family legend and a headliner on the campfire story circuit. If you have a *somebody's uncle* who shows up on your doorstep every Thanksgiving and who then leaves you with storytelling material to last till the next Thanksgiving, you get what I mean.

Within my stories, some lives take pages, others paragraphs. That's not an indication of the richness and value of that life, more a matter of how much of their story was passed from one generation to the next.

Speaking of the value of lives, I have a confession. In all those years of listening to and reading my students' Vietnam War era stories, I never shared one of my own. And I have one. It's about my cousin Johnny, and a long-overdue testimony to his ultimate sacrifice. For when he came marching home, there was no hearty welcome – only indifference. And in some of the ugliest moments of that era – loathing. You'll find it in the "War Stories" chapter.

As a young girl, I had the privilege to sit at the foot of several amazing storytellers as they wove their tales in captivating detail. When you've had that experience you know why the storytellers of ancient tribes were so revered. Not only did their bright visions chase away the dark nights, their stories ensured that entire cultures wouldn't disappear into nothingness, like a snowflake caught in the north wind.

When we allow ourselves the time to listen to the stories of those still with us; when we search out and pass on the stories of those who have died, we acknowledge that those lives matter. We anchor ourselves in space and time. And we unroll a tether that stretches both forward and backward to infinity.

It is my hope that you become inspired to tell your own stories. I know you've got them. Everyone does. And, if you're lucky, you may even have your own Charles.

COLLECTING AND FORMATTING YOUR STORIES

In the construction of my family history, you'll notice that I didn't use a chronological Abraham begat Isaac format.

Dry. Dry. Dry.

Rather, I chose to tell my stories in thematic chapters. I suggest you do the same. They don't necessarily have to be the exact same themes as mine, although you're more than welcome to use them. With themes, you can plug in stories from any era or ancestor that fits. And, if you only have a few stories for the theme, that's okay. Your chapters can be short or long. The idea is to get the stories down.

In constructing this book, I include excerpts of a few of the stories from my family history. In the original, many of my stories are much longer and more detailed. In the recording of your own family history, don't be afraid to be long-winded. You conducted the interviews, and did the research. This is your chance to get it all down. The generations that come after you want to know from whom they came in every gory or glorious detail. I include my story excerpts to ignite your memories; to act as a style guide; to illustrate my advice on writing and formatting your own stories; and to entertain you.

There is more advice on collecting and organizing your family history in the "End Matter" and "Resources" chapters of the book. There you will find suggestions on how to create family trees and family group sheets; samples of ways to share the fruits of your research with family members; methods of publication; how to organize photographs; and a list of resources.

To protect the privacy of the more recent generations of my family, I use first names only. For ancestors from generations so long ago that they have dozens of decedents, I use their whole names. They could be one of your relatives, even. Who knows?

Let's get to it!

1

PORTALS TO THE PAST

Growing up in Southern California in the fifties, the newly opened Disneyland was on every child's wish list. But for my E ticket, the best Adventureland ride around was my great-grandparents' Hollywood bungalow.

My maternal great-grandfather, who everyone called Grandad, was an adventurer extraordinaire. He collected mementos from every fork on his path. And they were not the kind you could fit in a cigar box. Rocks, bells, and bone fragments cast into diamond and square-shaped cement blocks framed his front garden. Steer skeletons and a wagon wheel rounded out the yard art. Rusty license plates shingled the entire garage. Inside the house, an ostrich egg, porcelain duck, and mouth harp decorated the mantel. And a plain white box that held the ashes of the love of his life, my great-grandmother, who we all called Bam, appeared in Grandad's gnarly fingers when he was in a pensive mood. All curious objects to an eight-year-old. And all of them carrying a story that Grandad was usually more than happy to share.

Some of the objects from the haunts of my childhood, however, came with stories not readily told by the owner. There was the green metal box in the hall closet of my paternal grandmother, Imogene. When you tipped back the lid it revealed the front page of a yellowing newspaper on which you could just glimpse a part of the headline, *Young Denver Couple Marriage...* Hmm?

My maternal grandmother, Marie, had her share of

yellowing newspaper articles stored in a sideboard drawer. One article had a photo of her hands; another a picture of her from a movie still with Fatty Arbuckle.

Other objects that fascinated me included: a frightening looking Maori warrior carved out of wood belonging to my paternal grandfather; a lapel pin in the shape of a tiny pill bottle that had belonged to my great-great-aunt; a handful of tiny uncut rubies that had something to do with a man with the exotic name, Abdu'l-Baha; and a crystal ruby vase that survived every one of the many moves my paternal grandparents made, and that always occupied a place of honor in their home.

Even now, one thing that fires my imagination as well as the ostrich egg is the correspondence that family members cherished enough to save. Posted from military camps and mines, business trips and holidays, most tell of that universal longing for the familiar when the traveler was immersed in a foreign and sometimes frightening experience. Those letters afford a real sense of the people that exchanged them. Reading them takes me as close to my ancestors' place in time as I can get.

Photographs take me there as well. After all, what collapses time better than staring at your identical eyes in a photo of your great-great-great-grandmother? Not so fun is discovering from the same photograph that in your old age you're face is going to morph into a cross between a hound dog and Whistler's mother.

I love contemplating portraits of ancestors from as far back as the early 1800s, but they do leave a lot of unanswered questions. I want to know: *What was life like for you? Who and what did you love? What were your strengths? Weaknesses? Did you have any fun?* Most of the relatives staring back at me from a hundred or more years ago look like they're sucking on a sour lemon drop.

Those photos make me hope for an eternity where I finally get the answers to those questions, and where I finally get to see their smiles.

In my family, we're very fortunate to have had two genealogists. My mother, Dixie, has devoted much of the last forty years to collecting our family history. With her almost photographic memory of names and dates and the stories that go with them, we know a lot about our ancestors. She originally conducted most of her research the old fashioned way – through libraries and the U.S. Postal Service. That means we have actual documents and letters you can hold in your hand – much more gratifying somehow than information staring back at you from a glass screen.

My paternal great-great-aunt Myrtle was the other genealogist. In the 1930s, she was so dedicated to her vocation that she moved directly across from the main library in downtown Los Angeles. She spent the next thirty years culling out every detail she could about her family, and did the same for clients. From her, we have volumes that she typed and bound. She also preserved artifacts and letters.

Myrtle only made one mistake, for which the family has not quite forgiven her. In her dedication to doing the responsible thing, she gave the History Society of Des Moines, Iowa a number of really cool family items. They include the Bible belonging to my paternal 4th-great-grandmother, which contains a record of family births and deaths lovingly penned by its owner. My parents visited those things while on a cross-country trip. They discovered that they *do not* hold a prominent place in the exhibit area of the museum, as we imagine Aunt Myrtle had envisioned. In fact, they aren't on display at all. No glory for Myrtle and the other branches of that tree. In order to see them, one must descend to the bowels of the museum and fill out a form. Then, and only then, a box dragged out from under a stack of other boxes is passed to you, so you can shuffle through your family stuff for a short period of time.

Historians and archivists, please skip the following paragraph.

Dear Reader: If you have any decedents whomsoever, don't do what Aunt Myrtle did. Give the museum *a copy* of those photos and letters and pages from the family Bible, if you're so inclined. *Keep* the originals, and *keep* the artifacts! I promise you, unless you've got the cup that George Washington kept his dentures in, once your stuff leaves your hands, it will never again see the light of day.

Your artifacts are your history. Label them, preserve them, and then pass them on down the line.

A bit of a neat freak, as much as I complain about messy attics, I'm really thankful to be descended from a family of pack rats. It's why I have a 130-year-old ostrich egg in my family room. My great-grandparents and their magical Hollywood bungalow are long gone, but there it sits, looking exactly as it did to eight-year-old me.

That ostrich egg, and the other artifacts, letters, and photographs are portals to the past and the people who lived it – an integral part of our family tapestry. As I connect with those things by touch or a long-ago memory, the stories of my ancestry unfold.

Here, then, is the first one...

THE RUBY VASE

As told by Enid, my cousin on my father's side.

My grandmother Elise, who I called Oma, was born in 1880 in Posen, in Germany. She spoke German. Education was very important to her, because she had not been allowed to go to school after her initial early elementary schooling. This lack was so profound that she complained into old age that her brother was allowed to go to school, but she wasn't because she was a girl. She insisted on having tutors in French and Italian for her young sons, William, my father, and Peter, my uncle. This resulted in them incurring the wrath of their teachers in their strict, anti-Semitic school. My father was punished for knowing the answers in French, "because he wasn't supposed to know that!"

Life became hard during World War I. My father was conscripted into the German army at seventeen and sent to the Eastern Front, where he was hit with mustard gas. In addition to the terrible PTSD he must have suffered, he also lost his sense of smell. As a teenager it used to frustrate me when I would get a new fragrance and ask him to smell how good it was. I was unaware enough to have to be reminded that he couldn't smell a thing. After the war was over, the borders changed. What had been the town of Posen became Poznan in the new Polish state. Jews were not welcome before, but now they were REALLY not welcome. The family fled to Berlin and

German citizenship.

My father moved away from Berlin, landing first in England, and then in America on an ill-fated trip around 1921. He didn't have sufficient funds to remain in the States so his visa was revoked. Back in Germany, by the early 1930s inflation gripped the country. He talked of taking suitcases of money to buy a loaf of bread. He eventually returned to England. When his visa was not renewed one year, however, he got his cousin, who was an Oxford don, to lend him the money for passage to America. His brother, Peter, and Peter's wife, Frieda, were already living in Detroit.

After traveling the U.S. for awhile, my father landed in Los Angeles. My mother, Irene, was living in New York and had come to L.A. to visit her family and her good friend, actress Margaret Hamilton, who was making a picture called *The Wizard of Oz*. Maggie threw a bingo party one night and invited both my mother and my father. Mother kept remarking that my father's name was familiar. They soon discovered they had a mutual friend in New York, whose apartment Mother had been subletting. It turned out that this same friend had met Oma in Italy. The woman couldn't speak Italian and my grandmother offered to translate for her. They became friends, and Oma eventually asked the woman if she would help her get letters to her son, who was living in the U.S. As her sub-letter, it became Mother's task to forward letters to my father in Los Angeles.

William and Irene were married six months later. It was 1939.

Things were getting very dangerous in Europe by this time. My father, Peter, and Frieda, who were also living in Los Angeles by then, worked diligently writing letters and contacting influential people to try and free Oma from Berlin. They finally succeeded, booking passage for her on the Trans Siberian Railroad, traveling east, with the United States as the final destination.

Most of Oma's belongings, including furniture, plates, silver, and other valuable items, had already been crated and shipped west. I don't know the story of how all those things managed to get to Los Angeles, but I do know that she had a ruby cut-glass vase that she had held back and hand-carried as she traveled by train and ship. It was supposedly on her lap the entire trip.

Her journey took her through Harbin, Mongolia, and Japan. After she arrived, my father interviewed her about the experience. One thing I remember from the account was her disappointment at paying for and not getting to see Moscow. The locked train on which she was traveling was shunted aside, delayed on one of the alternate railroad tracks. The Jews were put in separate train cars with covered windows to disguise their escape. But she was angry, because she wanted to see Moscow!

The dangerous nature of the trip didn't faze her as much as it does us in hindsight. I do know that when she arrived, according to Aunt Frieda, she was quite broken and emaciated. Frieda said Oma gulped her food down like people were going to take it away from her.

I assume that my Auntie Imogene was married around that time in Los Angeles, because Oma hand-carried that ruby vase all the way from Germany to give to her as a wedding present. Auntie Imogene ultimately gave it to me, saying that I was the one who should have it.

Oma lived until 1968, having witnessed the invention of electricity, the telephone, television, and air travel.

Now, go on your own ostrich egg hunt! One of the best things to build a story around is a tangible item that has significance to you.

Use letters, diaries, and photographs to spark your imagination and include in your stories.

Not all the stories must be told by you. Notice this first one was told by my cousin.

2

ROYALTY FROM WHOM
I MAY OR MAY NOT BE DESCENDED

*In my family history, I included a family tree chart for every branch of my family – similar to the model tree chart in the "End Matter" chapter. I ended up with nine of them. I placed them in the front of the book, right after the Table of Contents, so my relatives could refer to them when reading the stories. One of the most important items on the tree charts is the number I assign to **every** ancestor. That is the way in which readers quickly locate a relative to find where they fit on the family tree.*

Note the birth and death years and tree chart numbers after the bolded names in the story below. As within this story, use the following method every time you introduce an ancestor: **Anne Smith (1520–1624)–146.** *The number **146** corresponds with Anne Smith's number on her family tree chart.*

You're going to have to complete your tree charts before you write the stories, or go back and fill in the ancestors' numbers after you've completed your stories and tree chart.

Although I include the names, birth and death dates in all the chapters in this book, this is the only chapter I include the ancestors' numbers, because I haven't included a corresponding family tree chart for them. I use them only as a way of showing you the method you should use in your book.

In my own family history, I only bold the names, etc. the first time a relative appears in it. But I continue to include their birth and death dates and tree chart numbers, because relatives often appear in more than one story or chapter.

Brush up on historical events that pertain to your story, and include a few lines or an introductory paragraph as background on the event.

Notice I use bullets for the list of knights at the end of the story. This is a great method for groups of ancestors that you want to include for whom there is not a lot of information.

When reading this chapter, keep in mind that this book is about getting your family stories down before they fade away. It endeavors to teach you how to write a story-centered family history. It is not a how-to on creating an officially documented ancestral tree chart. The story below is meant to be a fun romp through the lives of people tied to me by threads of linen, not steel.

Pay attention to my disclaimer. I may or may not be related to Robert the Wifebeater.

In researching ancestral biographies on the various genealogy websites, you often come up with names and dates with question marks behind them. You also find the wording, "Not Proven," and comments like, "If she's supposedly so-and-so's mother, she gave birth when she was nine!" In some instances, arguments are made for and against an ancestor's entitlements, and/or involvement in historical events.
If it's really, really important to you to prove that you're a

descendent of one of the Surety Barons who signed the Magna Carta, I get it. There are a lot of perks that come with that. Who wouldn't want to put on a goofy hat and grab a front-row seat at a Royal Wedding?

Me, actually. And a lot of other Americans, I suspect. Our forefathers and mothers gave their lifeblood almost 250 years ago for us to not have to wear those goofy hats, remember? Or, rather, to never ever have to bow before royalty.

Historical accuracy is critical. Yes. But the further you travel down that ancestral road, the fuzzier the signs become. If you want to claim one of those Surety Barons or royalty from other countries as your own, you should probably hire a genealogist from the other side of the pond. "Proven" stamps take a lot of research and painstaking translation from derivations of languages long-since used.

If you'd rather just glean your family history from the genealogy websites, forgiving a question mark here or there, then go for it. Just be sure to qualify your stories with something like, "This is not officially proven, but three different websites list the same information for this ancestor." The internet never lies, right?

My ancestors from this chapter are down that road with the fuzzy signs. And because there are Surety Barons, Royal Mistresses and Conquerors in the mix, I'm highly aware that I won't be receiving a Royal Wedding invitation unless I hire a researcher to prove it. That's not going to happen.

So, here's my disclaimer: The royal branch on my ancestral tree begins with **Captain John (1609-1694)–118**, a solidly documented maternal multi-great-grandfather. From there, the limbs are a little shaky, mostly because they're supported by his grandmother, **Anne Smith (1520–1624)–146,** granddaughter of **Henry Skipwith (1539–1588)–149,** and **Jane (c.1535–1598)–150**, descendants of brave knights, royal mistresses, land barons, and the occasional mortician.

Can you guess what the Anne Smith issue might be? You're right. There are thousands of them, particularly if you throw in the Anns and Smyths. (You Smiths do have a lot harder job of tracing your tree than, say, the Moneypennys.)

I choose, however, to ignore the doubting Thomases, and claim my Anne Smith. For what writer could turn her back on stories woven of castles and kings, mistresses, and traitors? Not I. Here are those tales...

THE TALES

We'll start with the knights. But, hang on. We need a short history lesson.

It begins with William I (1028 – 1087) Duke of Normandy and First Norman King of England. In his lifetime he was known as William the Bastard, the son of unmarried Robert I, Duke of Normandy, and his Royal Mistress, **Herleva Falaise (c.1003-1050)–191**. It was only after his death that he became known as William the Conqueror.

William would have stayed the Bastard, too, had his cousin King Edward the Confessor been as saintly as his title suggested. Edward had told William he would name him king. He broke that promise on his deathbed, however, when he instead named Harold Godwinson, a powerful earl.

None too happy at the turn of events, William amassed a fleet of ships, gathered his faithful Norman allies, and headed across the channel to conquer merry old England. On October 14, 1066 he defeated and killed Harold at the Battle of Hastings. After a few more successful military encounters, William was crowned King of England on Christmas Day in London. Good thing, too. Somehow King Harold doesn't have the same ring.

Another good thing for the Crown and eventually historians and genealogists was King Williams' 1086 order of the "Great Survey," better known as the *Doomsday Book*.

The survey was an audit of all the taxes owed during King Edward's reign. Once an assessment of holdings and value was made, it could not be appealed. With that iron-clad document William claimed the Crown's rights, and was able to redistribute the land. The Norman nobility that faithfully fought with him in England were the recipients of that land. Castles went up. Clergy was altered. The political, religious, and physical landscape of England was forever changed.

That's where my knights come in. Oh, and William too.

It turns out that William I and my ancestor, **Robert, 2nd**

Earl of Cornwall of Mortain (1031–1090)–188, were half brothers. Robert supplied William with 120 ships for the invasion of England and was known to be with his brother at the Battle of Hastings. For that, William granted Robert 797 manors, including basically all of Cornwall. A little overkill for someone who, along with William, spent the majority of his life on the Continent.

I'd be a little more excited about my link to Robert if he hadn't been purported to be a really dense dude who beat his wife.

Robert's mother, Herleva, on the other hand, I'm delighted to claim. That is, with a heavy dose of disclaim, for hers is a legendary life cloaked in conjecture.

The following is the story still told by the tour guides at the Castle Falaise...

Herleva was born to **Fulbert de Falaise (0978–1022)– 192**, mortician (or perhaps a tanner, or both), and his wife **Doda–193**. Ruler of the castle and all the land was Robert the Magnificent, the young duke of Normandy. Don't you just love that title! He had to have come up with it himself when he was about thirteen. Watch for his character in the next *Avengers* movie!

One day, while surveying his kingdom from the castle ramparts, Robert spotted the beautiful Herleva in the courtyard below. Her task for the day was to trample barefoot on the garments soaking in dye in the stone dyeing trenches.

Aware that Robert was looking down at her, Herleva lifted her skirts higher than necessary to entice his interest. It worked. As with all the women whom he lusted after, Robert sent word that Herleva was to come to him through the back door.

Herleva would have none of it. No back doors for her. No way. If he wanted her, it would have to be through the front gate on a horse, and not as a commoner. Or else he could forget about ever seeing those shapely legs of hers again.

Charged with desire, Robert agreed. A few days later, the courtyard buzzed with the gasps and the gossip of the citizens of Falaise. Dressed in the finest garments her father could provide and astride a white horse, Herleva rode through the front gate, her head held high.

Duly pleased, the magnificent Robert named her Royal Mistress. No longer a commoner was she.

The two gave birth to William the Bastard. Whether they were ever officially married is still up for debate. The Bastard title makes me inclined to think not.

To secure the allegiance of a powerful ally, Robert eventually married Matilda, from the neighboring county of Flanders. Still in love with Herleva, however, he offered her up to one of his best buds, Herluin de Conteville, Vicomte, seigneur of Conteville. (Squeeze that onto the bottom of a check!) Kind of a funny way to show your love. Robert must have rationalized the deed by convincing himself that Herleva would be well taken care of.

We can't know how Herleva felt about it. But we can guess. As someone who insisted on riding through the castle's front gate, she probably didn't appreciate being traded off like a prize filly. And she no doubt started to question her fate when Herluin came down with leprosy.

Herleva and Herluin made a life, however, giving birth to two sons. One of those was my aforementioned ancestor, Robert the Wifebeater.

The history goes that Herluin's leprosy inspired him and Herleva and/or his second wife Arlette to found the Abbey Notre-Dame de Grestain. He and Arlette are buried there, and perhaps Herleva also.

Thus is my connection to William I. Yes, oh relatives of mine, if the Anne Smith link stands, you do share DNA with William the Bastard Conqueror. But no, not with the Robert the Magnificent. It's Robert the Mean Dimwit for us, I'm afraid.

Back to the knights.

There are quite a few of them on our family tree, recipients of lands and titles handed down generation to generation from William I's original distribution of lands. Which all sounds rather cushy until you read the fine print.

If you've got stuff, whether it's the best cave, hunting ground, or property and riches, generally speaking there's somebody who wants to take it from you. The history of mankind in a nutshell, right?

In that age, it was the knights' job to protect property and serve their sovereign. They didn't send the pages and squires off to do the dirty work for them, either. They were right there on the front lines, fighting off Danes and Scots, invaders from far and near. They were also on the front lines for intrigue and infighting, which on occasion made them enemies of the Crown.

It was not a job for the faint of heart, knighthood. William I himself died in September 1087 during a campaign in northern France.

Here are some interesting tidbits about a few of my knights...

- **Walchelin de Ferriers' (c.?–1040)–196** Hatred for his fellow Norman, Hugo de Montfort, was so great they fought to the death.
- **Alan Bassett (1158–1233)–176**, Counselor to King John, was one of the witnesses to the meeting with the Surety Barons, 15 June 1215. It was there the barons offered to trade King John's signature on the Magna Carta for his neck. Oh, to be a fly on the wall of that meeting! Bassett's name appears in the preamble to the Magna Carta along with the other kings' counselors. He was also at the accession of Henry III to the crown, and a witness to the reissue of the Magna Carta. What a life!
- **William de Montegue (1275–1319)–168** must have really impressed King Edward. For he not only supervised the shipping in the Scottish wars, he also suppressed the revolt of Llywelyn Bren in Glamorgan, Wales, and settled disputes between the people of Bristol and the town constable. In addition to his material rewards, he was granted the marriage of Joan de Verdon, an heiress, which he passed on to his son. Like Herleva, I'm not sure what Joan had to say about that!

- **Sir William Montegue (1303–1344)–166**, confidant of King Edward III, died at Windsor Castle of injuries inflicted at a tournament. They took their games seriously!
- **Sir John Montecute (1327–1390)–162** was beheaded for conspiring against King Henry IV.

Whether those fuzzy signs of my royal ancestry ever come into focus, it has been jolly good fun to wander into the world of clashing swords, fair maidens and, not the least, the birth of the Rule of Law – the Magna Carta.

3

IMMIGRANTS
COMMONERS FROM WHOM IT CAN BE CONFIRMED
I WAS DESCENDED

Notice that as with the chapters themselves, I chose to group the stories of my immigrants in themes. You may want to use chronological order instead. It is a much simpler format. Or you may have a good time coming up with themes of your own.

In this chapter are stories in which I include conversations and scenes that take place only in my imagination. I highly recommend allowing yourself to get so caught up in the lives of your ancestors that you hear their voices in your head – that you feel their triumphs and sorrows.

There is a reference to Find a Grave *in the story on John Proudfoot. You will find information* on Find a Grave *in the "Resources" chapter.*

The Beeler story explores the problems that can arise with multiple spellings for the same surname, and for same-name confusion on first names.

Notice that I lumped together the immigrants who sought refuge from religious persecution. Their stories are told in much greater detail in my family history book. I lead in to those stories with brief explanations about the religions. You may want to include a brief history about the events that were the catalyst for your ancestors' migration – potato famine; economic collapse; war...

Notice, finally, that I included the source for a quote on the Hempstead Convention in the last story, as I do in subsequent stories where I have taken something directly from a book or article. Your readers may want to look further into these sources.

When I consider my ancestral immigrants it's always with the same questions: Why did you leave? What forces led you to put your children on a boat that didn't look safe enough to cross a bathtub, let alone dark and angry seas? Where did you find the courage to turn your back on family and friends and wave good-bye to the familiar?

After studying their lives and times, it's no surprise that the answers for my immigrants are the same as for all immigrants over all time. The same – but definitely not singular.

They were driven by war, oppression, religious persecution, hunger, survival, money, greed, fear, love, adventure, itchy feet... Then there were...

THOSE WHO LEFT TOWN IN A HURRY

My Hart family from Stratford-on-Avon, England fall into the last category. I love this story! Apparently handier with tankards than plows, in their efforts to irrigate their own fields, they flooded the homes and land of all their neighbors. Considering the circumstances, they thought it best to vacate their premises and hop the next vessel out of there to the New World. I'm so glad they did, too. Because that definitely wasn't the last of the colorful Hart escapades.

My paternal 5th-great grandfather John Proudfoot (1752–1823) was an immigrant whose leaving was as much about running away from something as toward it. When John was a young man in Lasswade, Scotland, his parents decided that he'd make a great Presbyterian minister. Fairly well-to-do, they provided him with the education for that vocation. The further he got into it, however, the less enthused John became. Then one day he informed his parents that he'd rather be a barber. The following conversation likely ensued. No surprise! It's pretty much the same conversation your neighbors just had with their son.

Father: "A barber! A barber! You're telling us you'd rather fluff wigs and snip hair than save souls?"

John: "That's right."

Father: "After all that time and money we put into your education! You've never wanted for a thing, and this is how you repay your mother and me? We won't have it, I tell you!"

John: "I'm an adult now. It's what I want. And you can't stop me!"

Father: "Where are you planning to do this barbering? The black hole of Calcutta?!"

John: "The colonies."

Father: "That wilderness! You won't survive a fortnight! And don't count on us to save you!"

John: "I'll be fine. It's what will make me happy, Father."

Father: "Happy?! Where'd you get the idea that life is supposed to be happy?! We're born. We work hard. We serve the Lord. And then we die."

John: "Maybe here in Scotland. But from what I've heard, the folks in the Americas are actually known to pursue happiness. I want to live in a place like that."

Father – shaking his head and turning away, grim-faced: "With those aims, you and the colonies will amount to nothing!"

John did leave for the colonies out of the Port of London on the ship Elizabeth, November 21, 1774. He also fulfilled his dream of becoming a barber. Settling first in Virginia, he was an acquaintance of George Washington. We can't prove it, but he may very well have been George's wigmaker for a time!

Soon the frontier beckoned and John headed for what is

now West Virginia. There he and his wife, Leanor Hitt (1762–1829), raised seven children while farming 100 acres just outside of Phillippi. He also was a miller and taught school.

Although of Scottish rather than Scotch-Irish descent – a population that helped settle the region – while tilling a life out of the hard Allegheny earth, John became all that was right and good about the folks of hillbilly country. And he proved his father wrong.

Both John's parents, John Proudfoot (1708–1788) and Margaret Aiken (1715–c.1780), and grandparents Patrick Proudfoot (1680–1740) and Janett Hunter (1680–1711) are buried in the parish cemetery in Glencorse, Scotland. I made that discovery on the *Find a Grave* website. It was one of those moments of gratitude for the unknown relative who posted the photo of Patrick's tombstone, and also excitement at finding physical proof of a life begun in 1680. The kind of moment that made me want to book the next flight to Scotland!

Despite having turned his back on the ministry, John still must have been a man of great faith, evidenced by the lives of his descendants. One in particular, his grandson and my paternal great-great-great-grandfather Jacob Proudfoot (1822–1899) serves as the perfect illustration of the vestiges of that faith.

While living in Phillippi, Jacob learned of a man who was sentenced to death for killing his young nephew. Jacob visited the condemned man to offer him religious consolation. In addition, on the day of the execution Jacob sat next to the man on top of his coffin as he was paraded through the streets to the scaffold. Accompanying him up to where the noose was suspended, Jacob prayed with and for him until the drop fell. The rope didn't hold. The hanging had to be repeated. So it was twice that Jacob escorted that man into death, his faith stronger than his fear.

Perhaps the gruesomeness of that punishment was finally too much for the town, for it was reported to be the last hanging that ever occurred in Barbour County, West Virginia.

THOSE WHO WERE SWINDLED

Where's Leonard?

An ancestor who took part in the Palatine Migration was my paternal 6th-great-grandfather Johann Geist (1695–1792) of Wurttemberg, Germany. When the agents came around his village, he must have been highly motivated to get his family out of there. For, his next move has me on the fence about the guy. I'm not necessarily calling him a swindler. I'm just saying he may have left out a couple of important details when he gathered the family to tell them about their forthcoming adventure.

Johann booked passage for his wife, three sons, and a daughter, and sailed out of Rotterdam on the ship Andrew. They docked in Philadelphia in 1737, and eventually purchased a farm in Morris County, New Jersey.

When I first read their immigration story, I thought, "Well that sounds like pretty smooth sailing." Not quite. It turns out that two of those sons, Simon Geist (1729-1820), my 5th-great-grandfather, and his brother Leonard (1739-?), upon arrival in America were bound to one Mathias Slaymaker of Strasburg, Pennsylvania. Yes. That's right. Their dad paid for the family's passage to the New World by selling them.

Can't you just hear the conversation between father and sons?

Johann – arms outspread as if embracing the grand city of Philly: "Well, boys, here she is. Your new home. And this, by the by, is Master Slaymaker. He'll be controlling your every move for the next seven years. Make us proud, and be sure to look us up when the whole indenture thing is over."

Simon: "But, but... how will we know where to find you?"

Johann: "We'll write. Tata for now!"

Leonard to his brother – eyes wide: "Toto, I've a feeling we're not in Kansas anymore." Or something like that.

By the way, Mathias Slaymaker is his actual name. Perfect for a tyrant, don't you think?

And perhaps he was. For the next mention of Leonard is in the Pennsylvania Gazette under the listing: *Runaway Servants, Convicts, and Apprentices!!* I'm not really sure if they

31

ever found Leonard. I hope not.

Simon hung in there, however, and in the end, he did all right. He married pretty little Mary Bachman (1745-1842) of Bart township, Lancaster, Pennsylvania, the daughter of one of the largest landowners in the county. They became farmers, raised ten children, and spent their entire lives right there.

I'm not sure if Simon and the family ever reunited with his folks. I'm hoping they at least got together for an occasional weekend of fun at the Jersey shore.

Where's Waldoboro?

Samuel Waldo has two Maine towns and a county named after him. A wealthy eighteenth century merchant, he sought to increase his coffers through land speculation. Purchasing a large tract in coastal Maine, he sailed for Europe to recruit settlers.

Mr. Waldo must have been a pretty good salesman. Offering up a life of glorious opportunity in the New World, he found approximately 1500 unwitting souls to take the bait. Around 260 of them from Germany arrived in Boston in September 1752, with 133 of them continuing on to what became Broad Bay, Maine a month later. Michael Rominger (1709–1803), my maternal 6th-great-grandfather, was among them.

Most of that group of Germans hadn't left to escape war or religious unrest. Their reasons, like Waldo's, were economic. Unfortunately, the recruits didn't fair nearly as well as the recruiter.

Dateline: Broad Bay (now Waldoboro), Maine

Walking the gangplank of the ship St. Andrew, the passengers wave a cheery good-bye to Captain Hood, shake off their sea legs and turn to get their first glance at their new home.

Hardly able to contain their excitement, they take a few moments to marvel at the brilliant colors of a New England fall. But only a few, for they have work to do. Scattering like drone bees, they explore their new colony – picking out sites for their homes, church, and commercial buildings.

And then it begins to snow. And snow. And snow. And snow.

One of the settlers is quoted as saying, "We get snow in

Germany, but this stuff?! And the cold off the Atlantic? Goes right to the bones!"

Finding no bakeries or butchers in Broad Bay, and realizing that they hadn't received a primmer on life in Maine, another settler is heard to say, "Uh, oh."

After suffering hunger and bitter cold the entire winter and spring, someone in Boston (I'm guessing not Waldo) finally takes pity on them. Supplies arrived in Broad Bay in July of 1753.

Michael Rominger and his family stuck it out in Broad Bay until 1770. Then having become acquainted with the Moravians in the colony, they moved with them to North Carolina, where they helped establish a settlement that they named Friedland. In 1780, Michael and his wife, Anna Catharina Anton (1717-1794), took Holy Communion with the Moravians and became congregants.

THOSE WHO PREFERRED NOT TO BE BURNED AT THE STAKE

Burning at the stake. For centuries, emperors, kings, priests, and parliaments thought it a dandy way to deal with heretics. In 1414 England, they even convened what is known as the Fire and Faggot Parliament (Best government name ever!) to pass the Suppression of Heresy Act. A faggot is a bundle of sticks, by the way. The act made the law enforceable by Justices of the Peace.

So basically, even local JOP, Barney Fifington, had free reign to set fire to anyone he decided had espoused a belief or opinion contrary to the Roman Catholic Church, and later, the Church of England.

With the threat of a fiery death for one's religiious beliefs, freedom of religion was the wind in the sails of many an immigrant ship. I have ancestors who were Puritans, Quakers, Amish, and Mennonite. Some of their stories include:

Puritan: Susan Wood Butterfield Mitchell (1590-1645)
Paternal eleventh-great-grandmother

Part of the Puritan Great Migration, she, her husband, and son Samuel by her first marriage left England in June of 1635 on the ship James with 100 other passengers. That placed them right in the eye of the Great Colonial Hurricane – August 1635 – one night before they were to land in Boston Harbor. By doing a Google search, I was able to find a description of the hurricane, written by Reverend Richard Mather, grandfather of Cotton Mather and a fellow passenger. This is an excerpt from his journal: "That night a hurricane struck the coast, tearing up trees, demolishing houses and scattering the ships in the harbors. The James lost all its anchors and was blown towards Piscataqua. When it was within a cable's length of the rocks the wind reversed direction and drove it back towards the Isle of Shoals, where it was almost dashed to pieces again. Fortunately, the wind again died. When the tempest had passed it was found that not a soul had perished, nor had any of the cattle been injured. The following day one hundred passengers, twenty-three seamen, twenty-three cows and heifers, three calves and eight mares disembarked."

Susan's luck didn't hold out for long. Her home in Concord, Massachusetts burned to the ground with all their possessions in the spring of 1636. That summer the family moved to Saybrook, Connecticut, close to where war had broken out between the Pequot tribe and their enemies, the Narragansett and Mohegan tribes, who were allied with the English. In early October, Samuel and several other men went to Six Mile Island to retrieve hay. Concealed by the tall crop, Pequots hid in waiting for them. When the settlers got close, they leapt up, arrows flying. All escaped to Fort Saybrook – except Samuel. They captured him, tortured him, and burned him alive. The area where he was killed is known as Butterfield's Meadow.

Quaker: Robert Penrose (1632–1677
Paternal eighth-great-grandfather

I thought it would be enlightening to highlight some of the historical events of Robert's time. This can be done for any era. The following is a list of just a few of the events:

1642 to 1651 – English Civil Wars I, II & III – in which hundreds of thousands of soldiers and civilians died of war-related injuries, accidents, famine, and diseases. Loss in population was 3.7% in England; 6% in Scotland, and 41% in Ireland.

1649 – Charles I was beheaded. See above.

1665 to 1666 – The Great Plague of London – killed an estimated 100,000 people – almost a quarter of London's population – in 18 months.

1666 – The Great Fire of London – burned 70,000 of the 80,000 homes. It also destroyed St. Paul's cathedral, eighty-seven churches, and most of the government buildings. There were only six recorded deaths. However, that number may have been a bit skewed. Records weren't kept on the poor and working class, and the fire burned so hot it likely turned many of the bodies to ash. Interesting side note: the fire started in a bakery on Pudding Lane.

Fortunately, Robert missed the last two events, having moved to Ireland in 1656. Unfortunately, the move didn't do him a lot of good. In 1675, by then a Quaker, he was committed to prison for refusing to take the Oath to the King because of conscience sake. He died in Ballykean, Co. Wicklow, Ireland.

Amish and Mennonite: My Beeler ancestors made their exit to the New World in the 1700s.

It is these Beelers who offer the perfect opportunity to slip in a couple tips on dealing with one of the greatest roadblocks to genealogy research – names. In the course of their migration, the Beeler name changed many times. The oldest spelling that I found on record is Beyeler. The First Federal Census of 1790 lists twelve heads of families in Pennsylvania with the surname Beeler – with eleven different spellings: Beeler, Bealer, Behler, Beler, Bieler, Bielor, Beelor, Bealor, Beiler, Belor, Bieller. Five more appear in other records: Beuler, Behuler , Boyler, Byler and, finally, Bayler!

The point of making your head spin with B names? If you insert an ancestor's name into a search box and don't find her on your first pass, play with the spelling – again and again and again.

So, to the Beilers. No wait, make that Beelers. I mean, Beyelers.

Jakob Beyeler (1687-1771), my paternal sixth-great-grandfather and Swiss-born pioneer, fathered a long line of Amish and Mennonite and non-Anabaptist descendants. He and his wife immigrated on the Charming Polly (I have also read that the ship was named the Charming Nancy) in 1737. Their son Christian Beiler (1727-1812), my paternal fifth-great-grandfather, was with them. My third-great-grandfather David Beeler, Christian's grandson offers another opportunity to explain why first names can be just as problematic as last.

There was a famous Amish bishop named David Beiler who lived during that same time period, whose father's name was Christian. My David Beeler's father was also named Christian. With all that evidence, the two Davids look to be the same man, even with the difference in the spelling of their surnames. But, I don't think so. The fact that the 1850 and 1860 censes of Allegheny County Pennsylvania list my David as a farmer makes it highly unlikely he also had time to be an Amish bishop. David and Christian are two mighty common names that can lead to cases of mistaken identity. That's where documents like a census make it a whole lot easier to figure out who's who. See my entry on census data in the Genealogy Website section of the "Resources" chapter.

I do think, however, that Jakob Beyeler is likely to be my ancestor. Proof: I found an out-of-print book on Amazon entitled Family History And Genealogy Of Pioneer Jacob Beiler (1698-1771) BEILER - BOILER - BYLER. Published in 1998 and written by Allen R. Beiler. Part of the book description reads as follows: "Over 500,000 persons can trace their roots to Amish Pioneer Jacob Beiler, Boiler, Byler. Pioneer Jacob came from Switzerland to America in 1737 with his wife and five children and helped establish the first Amish community in America..."

I thought about buying the book until I noticed the used book price was $647! I'll just take Mr. Allen's word for it, and follow the logic that since Jacob had a half million descendants, Jakob and son, Christian, must be smiling down at me from a branch of my family tree. That is, if they're the smiling type.

Just three more comments:

We've got Yoders in the mix, too. I'm not sure you can even claim to be Amish if there's not a Yoder or two in the family.

Did you notice Allen's book title? Even he had a B-name issue.

And – really?!! 500,000 descendants?!! Is that even possible?

THOSE WHO FOLLOWED THE MONEY

In most of the previous stories, my ancestors fled from the dark figures of war, famine, and oppression clawing at their backs. Leaving was often quite literally a life or death decision. In the following stories, it was the dreams that hovered in front of my ancestors, not the beasts behind them, that drove them to immigrate. In America they recognized the light of opportunity and leapt for it. Stories of ancestors who immigrated for financial reasons include:

Anthonius deHooges (1620–1655)
Paternal eleventh-great-grandfather

He sailed to America as part of the Dutch West India Company, and settled in Rensselaerswyck, in what is now Upstate New York. The following is the type of historical information I often include in the stories: In an interesting side note, Rensselaerswyck was the only successful patroon settlement. The land stayed in the Rensselaer family for two hundred years. By the 1840s they were thought to be the tenth wealthiest family in the United States. Their tenant farmers were a tad further down the economic scale, and not one bit happy about it. Fed up with a feudal system that left them impoverished, they successfully petitioned against the system. And the land was sold. Which is the perfect opportunity for me to insert one of my all time favorite quotes by one of my all time favorite writers, F. Scott Fitzgerald – from *The Great Gatsby*: "Americans, while occasionally willing to be serfs, have always been obstinate about being peasantry."

Yet another great Google search find was that Anthony kept a journal that is held at the New Netherland Institute in Albany, New York. A biography of and the translation of his journal may be downloaded from their website. In the introduction, it states: "De Hooges's life and family history captured the imagination of previous generations of researchers. In fact, one such researcher went so far as to proclaim that there was 'probably no more picturesque a personality in all the colonial records.'" It is also regarded as a wealth of information about travel between the Netherlands and the colonies.

I cover quite a bit of Anthony's life in my book. One of his most enduring legacies is a small mountain that lies on the Hudson River between Westchester and Putnam Counties, which is named Anthony's Nose. That would lead one to the conclusion that his must have been a doozy.

4

CALLINGS
MAKING A LIVING – BUILDING A LIFE

*This chapter, which is built around working life, begins with the stories of two women. This is a good point to say that in the past women have often been left out of both oral and written history. I can assure you, however, they were there, and all-in. It would have been a bit problematic for humanity to move forward without them. Be sure to keep **her** story in mind as you're recording your family history.*

I use sub-themes in this chapter in the same way I did for the previous chapter. I only include a few of the stories. For some that I did include, I only gave a brief explanation of the subject matter. The important takeaway is that an hourly wage earner's job can be just as interesting as that of a CEO, maybe even more.

In the story of my maternal grandmother, I incorporate a newspaper article about her. The last story was gleaned from my great-grandfather's diary. If you are lucky enough to get your hands on diaries or news articles, be sure to incorporate excerpts into your stories. They add voice and validity.

THE CALLING FOR WHICH THEY AWARD
NO MEDALS

Check out the official portraits of Kaiser Wilhelm I and II and it may give you a good indication of why many Germans weren't too keen on their leaders in the last part of the 19th century. There's more fringe on their uniforms than Aunt Sophie's lamp. And their medals? What acts of bravery did they perform to earn those? Eating a ten course meal whilst at the same time bombastically showering their dinner companions with claptrap and spittle? And I won't even go into their handlebar mustaches and eagle-topped helmets. Except to wonder if perhaps the sour looks on their faces could have anything to do with the weight of said helmets. That could make anyone a tad cranky.

To those mustachioed Kaisers, add a poor economy and letters from family and friends extolling the opportunities awaiting in America. Then throw in enticing advertisements from steamship companies, and it's easy to understand why over 1.5 million Germans left their homeland in the 1880s alone. As a side note, even Wilhelm II himself left Germany by 1918. But then, there was the small matter of his being forced to abdicate and flee to the Netherlands. I wonder what ever happened to his helmet?

My maternal great-great grandparents, August (1851– 1912) and Maria (1850–1937) and their five children were among those who emigrated. In 1888, they booked passage in steerage and sailed for New York. Upon arrival, they moved immediately to Milwaukee, Wisconsin and then a year later to Kenosha. Both places had huge German populations. At that time, Kenosha supported six German language publications.

The family came from Berlin, where August had earned his living as a brew master on Unter den Linden Boulevard. It isn't *his* livelihood, however, with which I'd like to begin. Rather, it's motherhood.

As I make my way through both the personal and collective history of the movement to and through this country, I can't help but be in awe of the mothers. For, while being tossed in the bowels of ships and the backs of wagons, they were also diapering babies, comforting toddlers, and nursing ailing sons and daughters, who often died in their arms. Add to that the effort to keep their family fed, clothed, and warm, and I am humbled in wondering if I'd have had the strength to do the same.

The mother I'd like to begin with is the aforementioned Maria, otherwise known by the family as Grossmama. If anyone deserved a medal for bravery, it was she.

There is little we know of Maria's parents. We do, however, know much about her sister, Carlotta. She's an ancestor so infamous that she tops my "Villains and Black Sheep" list.

When Maria was six, she contracted measles. Carlotta, having learned that people with measles can go blind by staring at the sun, dragged Maria outside. She then forced her to look up into the sun, holding her there long enough to blind Maria for life!

A sweet soul despite being brutalized by her wicked sister, Maria grew into a lovely woman. August fell in love with her, and the two planned to marry. On the eve of their wedding, however, Carlotta took a knife to Maria's wedding dress, and slashed it to shreds! The woman really did belong in a Stephen King novel – either that or the fires of Hell!

Fortunately, Carlotta stayed behind in Germany. If she'd been Austrian, I may have been tempted to tell you she spawned Hitler. If you dwell on her too much you're likely to have nightmares.

All five of Maria and August's children were born before they left for America. That meant Maria navigated not only the voyage, but the move from New York to Milwaukee with a one, three, four, seven and nine-year-old in tow – without her eyesight.

When they finally arrived in Kenosha, Maria kept a loving home, raised her children, and was a wonderful partner to August. August and their sons, August, Jr. (1885-?) and Arthur (1879-?), worked in the Simmons Factory there in Kenosha. My great-grandmother, Martha (Bam) (1881–1962), was a knitter in the Allen A Hosiery and Underwear Mill. Her sister Emma Beth (1884-?) worked as a waitress, and her sister Olga (1887-1903) was a stenographer. With those sources of income, the family was able to buy a home and fulfill the dream they had for their life in America.

Sadly, it wasn't all smooth sailing. Olga died of a brain hemorrhage at the age of sixteen – with Maria at her side. Maria would go on to outlive August by twenty-five years, and August, Jr. by eight years. Those deaths were heavy burdens that she bore with grace – the grace of motherhood.

Another woman who managed both the tragedies and joys of motherhood with strength and grace was Inge (1895–1985), my maternal grandmother's au 'pare, and lifelong family friend. She is an example of one of those "relatives" I mentioned in the introduction with whom we may not share DNA, but who enriched our lives with their grace.

Inge worked as an au' pare for the family while attending the University of Colorado in Boulder, where my great-grandfather had his law practice. After receiving her teaching certificate, Inge taught first in a sod hut school in Flagler, Colorado, and then in a rural school in Kirtley, Wyoming.

It was in Kirtley that she met her husband, Arthur (1888–1984). Their story is the quintessential pioneer tale of the rugged Western frontier.

Art's parents homesteaded 1,700 acres in the eastern part of the Wyoming Territory. One of ten children, when he was young Art had no desire to be a rancher like his parents. Instead he took up bronco riding, becoming one of the most renowned cowboys on the rodeo circuit. To his dying day he was remembered as having successfully ridden a three-year world champion bronc, I-Be-Damned, at the Cheyenne Rodeo, and Lightning Creek, a three-year State Champion bucking bronco.

Art had envisioned for himself the free-wheeling life of a bronco buster. It was not to be. When it was time for his parents to pass the family ranch on, it came down to a choice between Art and one of his four brothers. They agreed that the decision would be settled by the flip of a coin. And the LOSER would take over the ranch.

Art lost.

How could ownership of a vast expanse of ranch land be considered a loss? Having been raised there, all the siblings knew the toll that the harsh land, isolation, and a lifetime of Wyoming winters could take on the spirit, never mind the body.

Growing the ranch from the original 1,700 acres, Art and

Inge eventually owned 6,000 acres. On it, at one point, they ran 350 head of prize Hereford cattle. For those acres and that cattle, however, they paid a great and miserable toll – the deaths of two of their four children.

When she was only three, their oldest daughter ate some poison that was used around the ranch. She died before they could reach medical help. Their twelve-year-old son died when he accidently shot himself with his own shotgun when he tripped over a barbed-wire fence. He too died before they could get him to a doctor. In my mind I have Inge holding both those children in her arms on a buckboard wagon, watching the life drain out of them as they made the long cursed journey into town. I don't know if that's exactly what happened, but whatever the scenarios, they must have been dark shadows hovering at the edge of Inge's vision her whole life.

The couple of times we visited the ranch, I was struck by tiny Inge's enormous strength of character. You could tell she believed life owed her nothing. Perhaps that's what helped her endure. The ranch house was a temporary shelter that Art had cobbled together decades before. It was always his intention to build Inge something better. But then there was that endless list of other things that needed minding or mending. She didn't complain.

Inge finally got her new place when their daughter and son-in-law took over the ranch and she and Art moved into an apartment in town. A grocery story near by; folks to talk to on the street – those were good times for Inge. And she certainly deserved them.

YOU MEAN THEY PAY YOU TO PLAY WITH BUGS? THAT'S SWELL!

This is the story of a great-uncle who was an entomology curator at a museum. Visiting him in his office full of pickled and pinned insects was one of my father's favorite pastimes.

YOU MEAN THEY SENT CASH THROUGH A TUBE? COOL!

This is the story of my mother's job in the tube room of a department store. Back in the day, a salesperson would accept cash for a purchase and then send it with the receipt through a tube and down to my mother who was waiting in the tube room. She'd make change and shoot it back up. Much more fun than a credit card! Plus, cash? You realize that means the shoppers stayed off the grid. There was no grid. No surveys. No hackers. No tracking your every move. Oh, to unravel what the 21st century has wrought.

THERE'S GOLD IN THEM THAR HANDS!

I found out about one of my maternal grandmother Marie's more colorful jobs from a 1920s yellowed and torn newspaper article she kept in the top drawer of her sideboard. The headline read, "There's Gold in Them Thar Hands!" And it involved one of her acting gigs.

The newspaper account of Marie's discovery begins like that of every other silent movie starlet. The only difference was that the discoverer was focused on her hands, not her face. The article states:

"Olga (her acting name), a Los Angeles Girl, was approached by a stranger two or three years ago. 'What marvelous hands!' he exclaimed. 'Are you working in motion pictures?' 'No,' Olga replied. 'Then, for heaven's sake, go see Dave Allen at the Central Casting Bureau! Register for work!' Olga went timidly to the Bureau and sought out Mr. Allen. He took one look at her long tapering fingers and hastily drew out a registration blank. 'There's plenty of work for you to do,' he said. (And so began her work acting as a hand double for actresses with knuckles the size of an ape's.)

"In a short while, she was called to one of the studios to spend a few moments before the camera holding up to view some letters and pictures. And a few days later she was called again to let her long fingers play idly over the keys of a piano. Then she was asked to raise the cuff of her sleeve and exhibit a wrist watch. That was all, and she was paid fifteen dollars in each instance. (A lot of money in the early 20s!)

"'I never go to bed without rubbing my hands with lotion,' Olga says. 'Hands need cream as much as the face, if you want to keep them soft.' (And now for my favorite quote from the article, for I heard her say this many times.) 'And don't drive a motor car. Gripping the steering wheel enlarges the joints. That's a warning!'" (And she heeded it, for in her entire lifetime her hands never touched a steering wheel.)

The article ends with: "Like the old prospector who exclaimed, 'There's gold in them thar hills!' these girls will tell you: 'There's gold in them thar hands!' And they exhibit bank books to prove it."

Marie's graceful hands and tapering fingers stayed that way her entire life. Fortunately, the hand gene was passed along to a few of the women in the family. When I see them, I think of young Olga flitting from studio to studio – on foot.

OCCUPATIONS THROUGH THE CENTURIES

These are written in chronological order.

As I look back over almost four hundred years of American history, many occupations have stayed the same; some job titles have remained unchanged, while their job descriptions have changed; and other occupations have ceased to exist.

I'm not sure how many **ferry boat operators** there are currently in the U.S., but my paternal 9th-great-grandfather Captain John Bissell (1591–1677) was arguably the first one. According to accounts of the Great Puritan Migration and the histories of early Windsor Connecticut, in 1648 John began a ferry service across the Connecticut River between the towns of Windsor and South Windsor in order to ferry cattle. So useful was the service that the Bissell family was granted a 150 year monopoly on the ferry.

The Captain John Bissell Memorial Bridge was constructed in 1958 and connects the towns of Windsor and South Windsor, a tribute to that first ferry service.

Sheriff is one of those jobs that you'd think would, for the most part, have been the same in the early 19th century as it is in the 21st century. If my maternal 3rd-great-grandfather

Leonard Ziglar (1792–1845) is any indication, that's not the case. Leonard served in the House of Commons from 1830 until his death. He was also a Colonel in the 2nd Regiment of the Stokes County, North Carolina militia, and presided over the Courts-Martial.

Leonard's main occupation, however, was High Sheriff of Stokes County, North Carolina. That's a title that demands respect, don't you think? Wrong! Turns out that with it the position required a rather extreme level of commitment.

As part of the job, High Sheriff Leonard had to pay the debt for prisoners who escaped under his watch. I don't know if he dozed off a lot on his shift or what, but quite a few of those convicts must have slipped away in the dark of the night. So many, that when Leonard died at only fifty-three, most of his estate went to the debt owed for the prisoners.

Do you suppose he read the fine print before they pinned a badge on him?

There's not a lot of call for **Vaudeville performers** nowadays. And that's too bad. The shows must have been a hoot! Comedians, singers, elocutionists... Small City USA residents lined up by the dozens when those acts graced their theatres. It was an opportunity to forget about the daily grind; to laugh, cheer, and to boo. And talk about power. In those pre-Yelp days, audiences had a much more effective weapon – the hook – and they weren't shy about calling for it!

My paternal great-great uncle Charles (1882–?) was one such vaudevillian. He and his wife had animal acts, including one that featured rats. A family diary entry states that Charles was paid $100 for a one-week engagement with those rats! We're fortunate enough to have photographs of Charles and his wife doing their poodle act. I doubt they got the hook much. Then, as now, there were a lot of dog people who probably loved watching puppies leap through flaming hoops.

So, it couldn't have been bad performance reviews. But for reasons that died with him, Charles left this world far too early, by his own hand. I like to think that when he reached the pearly gates, Charles was greeted by a pack of cheerful pooches and a rat or two, who kept the angels smiling with their antics.

I would be remiss if I failed to mention one last ancestor, my paternal great-great-grandfather Sydney (1844–1918). From the diaries of his son-in-law, Harry B, my great-grandfather, we gather that Sydney spent his working life one carousel horse shy of grabbing the golden ring.

We have photos of his splendid home in Denver, so we know that he did well for himself and his family. But from my great-grandfather, we gather that Sydney was never quite satisfied. Two careers he held were Superintendent of the City of Denver Garbage Department and original owner of the Denver Dry Goods Company. Denver Dry Goods went on to achieve great success under the subsequent owners.

Harry B's 1905 diary brings up two other enterprises and a revealing look at what he thought of them and Sydney:

Regarding **the Banana business***:*

Thursday, January 5

Sydney writes us about his Honduras trip. He has left a package at the Denver National Bank to be delivered to no one except me in case of his demise. Contrary to his intentions, he has paid in $2000 (about $55,000 in today's dollars) *to the Sula Valley Plantation Company before visiting the property.*

Friday, January 6

Everything is a bustle getting him off. While I think there is probably money in the banana business and Mr. Reed (Sydney's business partner) is associated with good men, morally and financially, the unfamiliar conditions are apt to discourage him with the enterprise quite early.

Thursday, January 26

In a letter from Sydney mailed at Puente Cortez upon his landing there, with the greater portion written aboard ship at Belize, he says, despite the experience of gales and rough weather, he has not been at all sick, and he has enjoyed the trip. He was evidently still sanguine of prospects and speaks of permanent habitation there. He has not seen the growing banana yet, but is confident of Reed's integrity and feels sure of the venture.

Thursday, February 2

Dora (his wife) *says she has received a telegram from Sydney from New Orleans, saying he will be home Saturday. We are surprised at his early return and do not know what construction to place upon it.*

Sunday, February 5

Sydney and his associates have decided to abandon the Honduras business, and 'at last he has found Reed out.' It seems strange that the discovery would not have been made earlier. (Hmm. You've gotta love the subtlety in that comment.)

Tuesday, February 7

Sydney writes that they found the chief drawback in Honduras to be want of transportation facilities. And likewise they concluded that Reed was not the man they could continue in business with; that they will all get the money they contributed; and Sydney and the other stockholders who made the trip will have their traveling expenses paid. He said the trip did him good, and he is glad he took it. (There is that.)

Regarding **the Barbershop business**:

Thursday, October 19

Sydney writes that he has fitted up a barber shop, the best in Denver, and is going to make money, and I must go down Sunday to help him draw his contract with his manager, a practical barber. What next!

Saturday, October 21

Reached Denver an hour late. Find Sydney has a fine barbershop and he was in the throes of an 'opening.' Charles (Sydney's vaudevillian son) *has a tailor shop in conjunction and it was through this means that Sydney became interested in the barber business, which is certainly the limit. I expect he will soon tire of this enterprise, just as all the others. It is his born nature to move by extremes: either heightened enthusiasm or intense despondency. I drew no contract for him, as the date was not yet available.*

Thursday, November 30

Thanksgiving Day! Sydney has sold out his barber business, at a sacrifice, as usual. A man whose enthusiasm overcomes his judgment very frequently.

5

WAR STORIES

In this chapter, as with several others, I include my own thoughts at both the beginning and the end. It's important for your readers to know who you are, as your book is part of your legacy. Hopefully, it will still be read long after you're gone. You may also want to include your own story in either the beginning or end of your book.

War stories work best in chronological order. I have included subtitles for all the wars in which my ancestors fought that I included in my family history, not necessarily the stories themselves. I include brief war histories for several of the stories.

One of my stories revolves around the Moore House, a noteworthy location in the history of the American Revolution. Places are often as interesting and significant to the lives of you and your ancestors as people. If you have a place of importance to you and your family, tell its story.

Notice that I called Park Rangers to verify some information about the Moore House. They were very helpful. Yes. The telephone is still an excellent tool.

Once again I would encourage you to use letters, diaries, and newspaper articles in your storytelling. Reading the letters of my ancestors who fought in these wars was one of the most heartrending experiences of my project. But, the most poignant was hearing the catch in my father's voice when he talked about his own experiences.

Don't leave out the folks on the home front.

*Remember to use your project to **interview** your family members – the greatest gift of all – to them, to you, and to all who come after you.*

The last story in this chapter takes place during the Vietnam War. If you can claim a war, I guess you could say that was *our* war – the Baby Boomers. In the 50s of our youth, raised on streets lined with regimental rows of ranch-style homes so new the air smelled of fresh paint and asphalt, life appeared *Leave it to Beaver* perfect.

The perception remained right on into 1963. And then things started to change: An assassination. The Beatles. Long hair. Go-Go boots. The Gulf of Tonkin incident. *And change:* Race riots. Mini-skirts. Anti-war protests. The Tet Offensive. *And kept on changing:* Psychedelics. More assassinations. Woodstock.

When I entered the ninth grade in 1966, the girls were still wearing pleated skirts and sweaters. The boys' hair was above their collars and their shirts were tucked in. There was a dress code. And it was enforced.

By the time I graduated in 1970, it was another world. The dress code was gone. The Greatest Generation was thoroughly disgusted with their worthless progeny. The country was thoroughly disgusted with a war without an exit strategy.

And in the course of all that, some of those very progeny were fighting for their lives, and they thought, for their country, in muddy rivers and dense jungles. One of the most frightening reasons their enemy was winning because they knew those jungles. The V.C. understood the advantage of unsophisticated gorilla warfare over mechanical might. Booby traps, tunnels, and knives. Combat without rules of engagement. We had them. They didn't.

What I learned through the interviews my students conducted for the Vietnam War project I mentioned in the introduction was that soldiers who fight the same battle don't come out with the same wounds – physical or psychological.

What I learned from researching the following stories is that from my ivory tower I have only the most distant view of what it's like to put your life on the line – to know that there's someone out there lurking in the shadows or looming in the skies above you whose mission is to kill you.

It is with humble gratitude I give you the stories of our family members, who fought to create this country. And then continued through the centuries to defend our freedoms and the freedom of millions on distant shores.

PRE-REVOLUTIONARY WARS

If you were one of the early colonists of North America, there was a very good chance you were involved in an Indian War. There were dozens of tribes east of the Appalachian mountains alone, with a long history of fighting between each other. Throw in the historical competition for power between European and British settlers; have the Natives desperately defending their tribal lands while being simultaneously decimated and courted by the warring whites; and you have the perfect recipe for massacres and mayhem. That is what is included in this section.

THE REVOLUTIONARY WAR

Our Revolutionary War Veterans

In this section I told a few longer stories, and then highlighted the rest of my ancestors in bullet points with their names, rank, companies, and battles in which they participated. I included stories of family members who were loyalists as well.

The Moore House

My maternal great-grandfather, Grandad (1876–1962), was one of the world's great storytellers. His own story is told in the "Golden State" chapter. One of his favorite claims to fame was that he was born in the Moore House, Yorktown, Virginia. To prove his veracity, when re-telling the story he'd present a key to the desk that sat in the entryway of the house. Famously, that is the home to which Lord Cornwallis referred when he sent General George Washington the following note on October 17, 1781: *Sir, I propose a cessation of hostilities for twenty-four hours, and that two officers may be appointed by each side, to meet at Mr. Moore's house, to settle terms for the surrender of the posts of York and Gloucester.*

Over the century following the Revolutionary War, the Moore House had many different owners. During the 1862 Peninsula Campaign of the Civil War, caught between Confederate and Union forces, it sustained a lot of damage by shell fire. Soldiers also tore siding off the house to be used as firewood.

According to its history it was from that time until 1881 that the house was described as derelict. It was also at that time that we do know my maternal 3rd-great-grandparents, William (1815–1888) and Maria (1819–1900), owned it. The York County deeds show that they purchased the 475 to 500 acre Temple Farm on which the Moore House stands in 1870 for $2000. They paid it off in April, 1881.

Their daughter Virginia (1851–?) was Grandad's mother. She was married to my great-great-grandfather Eugene (1849–1928). His parents had been sent to Yorktown to help maintain the peace after the Civil War. Eugene was living there with his parents when he was twenty-one, as he is listed in the 1870 Census with the occupation of farm laborer.

We know that Grandad lived in the Moore House when he was a young boy, as his father Eugene was the manager of Temple Farm at that time. He was not, however, born there, as evidenced by his birth certificate, which states his place of birth as Charlottesville, Virginia.

We did see a desk in the entry of the house when we toured it in the 1990s. Whether Grandad's key fit it, we'll never know. It disappeared with his death.

Possessing photos of William and Maria, and knowing their status in their home community of Baltimore, Maryland, I have no idea why they'd allow the home to deteriorate. They manufactured windmills on East Pratt Street and had a fish business on Bowley's Wharf, South Street. I don't see Eugene allowing that to happen either. Maybe it was just temporary housing for him and Virginia and their young family while his in-laws were deciding what to do with the farm. You'll read much more about those two in the "Golden State" and "Villains and Black Sheep" chapters. Oooh.

The good news for the house was that in preparation for the Centennial Celebration of the Patriot victory at Yorktown in October, 1881 the house was refurbished. The rangers at Yorktown Battlefield National Park said that they are pretty certain my ancestors sold the house to the Centennial Commission at that point. Later, between 1931 and 1934, the National Park Service completely restored the house back to its original colonial design

And Then There are the Deserters...
Or... *It didn't pay to be good-looking or to be in charge of the teapot.*

Michael Rominger (1709–1803) Maternal 6th-great-grandfather
Although in the Colonies during the Revolutionary War, he left his military service behind him in Germany. From his memoir:
"A native of Winterlingen, Germany, Michael was a Lutheran who worked as a journeyman carpenter. Large and handsome, he was called at the age of twenty-five to become a soldier in a Royal Regiment. After three years, he became weary of the life. When he couldn't secure a discharge, he left secretly and went to his parents. Fearing he would be caught and taken again for service, his parents sold their homestead and moved to Siegen, Germany. There he supported his parents as a carpenter."

Johann Adam Henning (1755–1824) Maternal 5th-great-grandfather

The British didn't have a large standing army, so when the American Revolution broke out, they looked to Germany. Several German princes were more than happy to fill their coffers by hiring out entire units of Hessian soldiers. The number of Germans fighting with the British eventually grew to close to 30,000. Incensed at the British for hiring a mercenary army, the Americans eventually offered 50 acres of land to any Hessian who deserted. Johann was among them, though there is no evidence that he received land. The accounts of Johann from various historical associations state that he came to America as an aide to General Cornwallis, and deserted on February 9, 1781, after the Battle of Guilford Courthouse, North Carolina.

From The Carolina Room ~ Forsyth County Public Library, Winston-Salem, North Carolina:

"An old story says that Adam Henning was in charge of Lord Cornwallis's commissary. On the way across the Yadkin he lost the Lord's favorite teapot. Fearing retribution, he deserted."

Johann eventually took refuge in the Moravian community of Bethania. As the Battle took place in North Carolina and involved Cornwallis, and as Johann lived out his life in Forsyth County North Carolina, the account seems accurate.

THE CIVIL WAR

"War, at the best, is terrible, and this war of ours, in its magnitude and in its duration, is one of the most terrible."
Abraham Lincoln

The death toll in the Civil War is estimated to be 650,000 to 750,000, over two percent of the population of the United States at that time. To put it in perspective, given today's population, the deaths would number over six million. The Civil War has been remembered as a war of brother against brother. Those families who lived on the borders between Confederate and Union states often sent sons off to war on both sides of the conflict. It was also, however, a war of brother *with* brother. Regiments were formed in communities, so men enlisted with neighbors and kin. It is devastating to think of brothers dying at each other's hands. But is it any less devastating to think of brothers dying at each other's side?

Below are the stories of the Civil War veterans from our family who fought with, and lost, the most precious of all things to them, a brother.

Cyrene VanScoy Proudfoot (1826-1911) Paternal 3rd-great-grandmother. The following are her brothers:
Aaron VanScoy (1834-1888) 6th Iowa Infantry. Mobilized at Chariton, Iowa
Jacob VanScoy (1840-1863) 12th Indiana Infantry, Co. D; Mustered 8/5/1862
James VanScoy (1844-1920) 12th Indiana Infantry, Co. D; Mustered 8/5/1862
Thomas VanScoy (1848-1901) Since he was too young to enter the army, he ran away to war and was returned home. He ran away again and served as a drummer boy. He finally enlisted in March of 1865, Company I, 154th Indiana Volunteers, 2nd Regiment.

The story of Aaron's, Jacob's, and James' Civil War service is told by them through their letters. They were preserved by their parents, my paternal 4th-great-grandparents, William VanScoy (1805-1887) and Mary Channel (1808-1878). Then they were passed down to their sister Cyrene, who gave them to her niece, Lillian. They ultimately ended up with Lillian's sister, the aforementioned Aunt Myrtle. She was the genealogist who tirelessly worked to preserve our past, even going so far as to type every word of these letters, along with hundreds of other documents.
The following are excerpts from those letters:
From Jacob – Grand Junction, Tennessee
February 25, 1863
Dear Father and Mother,

It is with the greatest pleasure that I sit to let you know that we are all well for which we are all glad. I was to see Aaron this morning. He is better. He was setting up. I think he will be able for duty in a few days. You need not be uneasy about him.

There was two (of the dead) taken up some time ago and the man got as far as Memphis and stopped to stay overnight. He went to bed with seventy-seven dollars, and he was found dead the next morning, with his money taken and the two corpses there.

What will this world come to? The wickedness of our nation is great at this time, and there must be a change before this war will close. But I think that the people begin to see the one thing needful. Well, father, I see that need of living in readiness for death at all times. I see men falling nearly every day, but I think that I will get home safe. But I can't tell. But one thing certain, if I fall, I expect to fall in sight of heaven. I am far from home and in the enemy's land. I feel that I have a friend that is with us in trouble, and if we put our trust in him, he will bring us off more than conqueror. Thank him who has died for our sins, and for praying parents.

Well, I think if I get home I will know how to appreciate the privileges that I once enjoyed. I don't feel discouraged. I feel willing to stay in defense of our country. The first charge of a soldier is to discharge his duty to God, and then to his country.

Well, as far as the war news, expect you know more about that than I do. But I don't think that it can last long... We haven't got our pay yet. There is four months past due us the last of this month.

Write to me as soon as you get this. I remain your child Jacob, to his much respected father and mother, Will VanScoy and Mary VanScoy.

From Jacob – Haines Bluff, Mississippi
June 17th AD 1863
Kind and affectionate parents,

It is the greatest of delight that I seat myself to let you know that we are all well and hope this may find you in good health... We have got a long ways down in dixey, but are not very uneasy but what we will get home before long. There is some that won't get home. We can't tell who they are.

We are at this great place they call Haines Bluff, about six miles from Vicksburg. We can hear cannon roar plain at Vicksburg. Grant has got them bound in so they can't get out, and he has got sharpshooters within 200 yards of them. When they poke their heads up to load thare cannons, there is a dozen pills, as we call them, sent at them. But our men keep thundering the shot and shell into their fort. They opened a space of two miles around them last evening to draw them out. They came pouring out and our force closed in on them with their artillery. Before they could get into their den, we mowed down a lot of them.

Well, I think that the place will soon be ours, for Grant is very steady and seems confident of our success. We are looking for Johnson and Bragg to attack us here every day. They say they have seven thousand troops, but they had better not try it with that force, for we have that many and enough to beat them in Vicksburg. We have the strongest position in the west and we are well fortified. The bluff is lined with artillery, and there is gun boats laying along in the river, thick enough to shell them on either side.

We are still in good spirits and look to the time when we will get to go home and stay. Don't be uneasy about us for we will try and take the best care of ourselves we can. We are signing the payrolls today. We will get two months pay in a few days. I sent 20 dollars home and never heard from it. I sent it before we left Collierville in a letter. This is the 13th and they are still pounding away at Vicksburg.

Write soon as you get this - direct as before. I will close by returning my thanks. Yours truly, Jacob VanScoy to W and M VanScoy.

From James – Athens, Tennessee
December 11, 1863
Dear Parents,

It is with a sad heart that I take my pencil in hand to let you know that Jacob is dead. You will doubtless think it strange of me not writing to you sooner, as I suppose that you will hear of the battle and probably of Jacob's death before this letter will reach you, but circumstances has been so it was impossible for me to send a letter.

On the 24th of last month we, the 15th army corps, crossed the river above Chattanooga and advanced on the enemy, driving them without much fighting until we drove them to Missionary Ridge. There we stopped for that day and early in the morning of the 25th we formed in line and advanced on them – our brigade on the extreme right of our corps. We marched in line of battle about a mile, when we came to a fence, which was at the edge of the woods and in range of the rebels' batteries on the ridge. There we was ordered to lie down and we lay there a short time, and then we was ordered forward, right out in an open field where they had 16 pieces of artillery firing on us and was also exposed to their riflemen. Jacob and I climbed the fence and marched up side by side. After we had advanced about 300 yards there was a musket ball that struck Jacob in the left breast, passing square through him. He fell by my side.

I dropped my gun, and by the aid of another man, managed to get him back to a ditch, which was close where he fell. There he pitched into the ditch. The man that was helping left me there. The ditch was so deep and narrow that I could not get him out. All I could do was to hold his head out of the water. There I remained 15 minutes – the shot and shell tearing the ground up all around me. I could look and see the rebels charging – one line after another – down the hill on our boys, who were about 200 yards ahead of me. And there – Oh, my God! What were my feelings? There lay my dear brother that I knew could not live long, and I did not know how soon our men would be repulsed and I would be forced to leave him to die in the battlefield. I saw some men close by. I hollered at them, and they came and assisted me in getting him off the field to where I got him in an ambulance and took him to a hospital.

I felt to thank God when I arrived at the hospital. It was then nigh sundown. I got some straw and laid him on it. After a long time I got a surgeon to examine him and he told me that he must die. It was about 15 minutes after that the Lord released him from his sufferings. He died at 10 o'clock and was wounded at noon.

From the time that he was wounded he suffered intensely, but thank God he died a happy man. Shortly after he was wounded, he told me while he was on the field that he had to die. I spoke to him about his soul, and he did not seem at first satisfied to die. But shortly, the Lord powerfully blessed him, and he was enabled to shout, although he suffered intensely. He took from his pocket a testament and gave it to me and told me to read it and meet him in glory. He also told me to tell his wife to train up his children in the nurture and admonition of the Lord and to meet him in heaven. He then said to tell father and mother and all the boys to meet me in heaven. He then wanted to see Aaron, and I sent for him, but he did not come until a few minutes after his death. I thank God he has gone to Heaven.

Oh, my dear parents, you have a son buried beneath the sod of Tennessee. But he rests in Jesus and will rise at the last day to meet us in glory if we but prove faithful.

The next morning, Aaron and I buried him (nicely) where all soldiers that fell there was, although we had no coffin. We dug a vault and lined it with boards and then inscribed his name on the trees that we buried him under.

By this time the regiment had passed and gone. I had to start in a hurry to overtake them, which I did that night. We drove the rebels down to Ringgold, Georgia, where after a pretty hard fight they was completely routed. And then we was ordered to reinforce Burnside at Knoxville, where we heard that Burnside had routed Longstreet. We started back to Chattanooga to get supplies, for we had been subsisting on the country ever since the fight. Now we have gone back as far as this place, which is about 50 miles from Chattanooga, and no rations yet. We are doing tolerably well. We are laying by today on account of the rebels burning a bridge across the Hiwassee River.

Well, my dear parents, I feel almost lost and without friends since the death of Jacob, but I hope that I shall be more faithful now to my God and country. Our company lost two killed and seven wounded; the regiment lost about 100 men killed and wounded. It was an awful hard battle, as doubtless you have heard. Our orderly sergeant was in the battle of Shiloh and several other hard battles, and he said that he never was in as hot a battle as this was.

I hope I shall never be called to witness another such a battle... I don't know what to do with Jacob's things. He lost nearly all of them on the battlefield, and I have what few things is left. I will sell and send the money to his wife as soon as I can, and will write her a letter. As soon as payday comes I will send all that is coming to him and send it by mail or express. You can inform her of the affair and I will write her a letter the first opportunity I have... As soon as I can I will write a few more words. No more at present.

Jacob died at Missionary Ridge at the Battle of Chattanooga. His remains were removed from the spot where his brothers buried him and he is interred at the National Cemetery in Chattanooga, Tennessee. In that battle, one of the Confederacy's two major armies was routed. The Federals succeeded in holding Chattanooga, opening a gateway to the Lower South and giving Sherman the logistics and supplies he needed for his 1864 Atlanta Campaign, in which Aaron and James fought.

From James
Battle line near Atlanta, Georgia
August 13, 1864
My Dear Parents,

As I feel somewhat comfortably situated this evening for writing, I will drop you a line to let you know I am well and in good spirits... The sickly season is now here and many of the soldiers are now sick, but a smaller portion than expected... I think now we have our established line and the probability is we will remain here until the enemy is flanked out of Atlanta. We are still on the front line within a few hundred yards of the enemy's main line of works. We are molested a great deal with sharpshooters. They make us lay pretty close to our ditch. In front of some other regiments they have made an agreement with the rebel skirmishers not to fire at all unless either side undertakes to advance.

If you have any spare reading matter, send me something to read.

The boys have their own fun with the rebs. They meet them half way and trade coffee for tobacco. Our boys here went so far as to go over inside of the rebel works to trade with them. And they have come over to our works after coffee. They seem very clever and give us good bargains in the way of trading. But in front of our regiment and the 99th Indiana they are more hostile. It seems they have a spite at us. At all times during the day they send their missiles of death over our works. When night comes the firing ceases and both sides maneuver all night to gain an advantage for the next day.

I was back to the hospital yesterday to see Aaron. He is about as he has been – poorly, but I think he will get along finely. I think if he takes care of himself that he will soon be able for duty. There is not many of our division back there sick. There is quite a number there wounded. Some now are dying every day, but a large portion of the wounded are but shot and they will soon be able for duty again.

The weather is extremely hot here... This is curious country here, We cannot tell ever hour ahead if rain is coming.

Well, I remember where I was two years ago today. It was the day that Company I first went into camp at Indianapolis... and the war is not ended yet. One more year and our time will be out and, oh, I hope by that time the war will be over.

I am still striving to live and serve the Lord, and I find that it is not a vain thing to serve him. He is a friend that sticketh closer than a brother. His grace is ever sufficient for us, and my only desire is to live for him and make myself useful to this end. I have resolved to fit myself for future usefulness should I be spared to get home. Pray for me. Write soon to your son, James.

James *was* spared to get home, in his own words: *Mustered out at Washington City on the 5th day of June 1865.* During his service, James participated in the battles of Richmond, Kentucky; Vicksburg and Jackson, Mississippi; New Hope Church, Kennesaw Mountain, Nickajack Creek, Atlanta, Jonesboro, and Griswoldville, Georgia; Columbia, South Carolina; and Raleigh, North Carolina. He lived to be seventy-six, dying of Typhoid Fever. Aaron died much younger at fifty-four, of Yellow Fever in Florida. I was surprised to hear that he was in the deep South, as miserable as he seemed to have been on the long trudge south to Atlanta.

There is no long list of battles in which youngest brother **Thomas** participated, not achieving his goal of enlisting until a few months before the war's end. However, with the same strength of character as his brothers, he dedicated his life to serving others, as a reverend and university president.

THE SPANISH AMERICAN WAR
THE BOXER REBELLION
WORLD WAR I

Included in my family history are several stories about ancestors who fought in the above wars. In the case of the Boxer Rebellion, I included a bit longer introduction, because many people are unfamiliar with the conflict.

WORLD WAR II

Born seven years after the end of World War II, like many baby boomers, my life was still very much influenced by it. The memories were fresh in the minds of the adults in my life, the nightmares still very real to those who fought.

My paternal grandfather, Link, was a Marine – a bigger than life man in both stature and personality. I knew him so well I can still feel and smell the rough wool of his Pendleton shirt from the last bear hug he gave me.

A football player at Santa Monica High School, his size and ability as a running back didn't go unnoticed. By the time he graduated in 1925, he had been recruited by the University of Southern California to play for them. It wasn't an invitation to attend classes, mind you. They just wanted him on the team, as they did also John Wayne.

According to notations in his mother's Bible, he enlisted in the Marines on June 30, 1926, and left for San Diego the following day at 2:30 p.m. His brother Lou enlisted three months later.

The first action he saw as a Marine was in Nicaragua. The U.S. had occupied it since 1912, trying to ensure that if a canal was dug there, it would be built by Americans. When civil war broke out in Nicaragua in 1926, the designated Nicaraguan president requested intervention from President Coolidge. Four hundred Marines arrived on January 24, 1927. By March there were 2,000 troops. America's attempts to broker peace, however, were unsuccessful. The U.S. pulled out of Nicaragua by 1932.

Link was long gone by then. He and Lou sailed to Shanghai on January 10, 1927. Known as China Marines, they and the other Marines were sent there to protect American citizens and property during a time of unrest between Chinese Warlords. We have a photograph of them marching with their regiment on the Bund. It must have been pretty exotic duty. It's said that the Marines fared well, with the ability to buy local goods very inexpensively and to mix with the partying expats – perhaps frowned upon by their officers – but something I'm quite sure wouldn't have kept the two brothers away.

Out of the Marines by 1930, one would have thought Link's military career was behind him. But then... Pearl Harbor.

He thought that at his age and due to his prior service, they'd give him a desk job. The Marines had other things in mind. He ended up in the 3rd Marine Division in the Pacific theatre. He fought in the battles of Bougainville from November 1943 to January 1944; and Guam, from August to October 1944. He only missed Iwo Jima because he had become ill from malaria and other tropical diseases. They put him on a hospital ship and sent him home. There's a photo of him in the jungle, shirtless. His ribs are pronounced, but so is his smile.

We are fortunate to have all Link's letters, photographs, medals, and mementos from the war. Through them, it's easy to get lost in time. Through them, one understands why the courage and tenacity and selflessness of that generation is so revered.

One of my favorite items is my grandmother Imogene's war diary. Slipped into it is a torn sheet of lined paper, with the title "Code for Letters" typed at the top. She and Link created it for her to know where he was once they shipped out. In those loose lips sink ships time, military personnel couldn't reveal where or when they were deployed.

The code includes:

Solomons... a party

Aleutians... property next door

Pearl Harbor... backyard

Met the Enemy... Saw Jimmy Hicks the other day.

They never had a chance to use it, so far off were they in their guesses as to my grandfather's assignment.

As with the Civil War section, Link's and Imogene's WWII experiences are best told in their own words. The following are excerpts from my grandfather's letters to my grandmother and from her war diary.

Link:

Camp Pendleton - Thursday Noon - February 1943

I'm dashing off this short note because I have just been notified that I am to go into Oceanside at 2p.m. on Company business. I'm suspicious of censorship and I want to add what I didn't know last night. It is reported (not officially) that there will be no liberty of any kind before sailing. In that event you'll

63

not be hearing from me. I think we'll sail this weekend. The letters from now on will contain no news of any censurable nature. If possible I'll call before departure, but I think our lines will be closed. Keep a light burning. Your lover and husband, Lincoln

Link:

March 1943

We arrived at our destination safe and sound. The trip was without mishap and everyone is in good health. Things here are not too bad. We have access to some Americana, including a few Bing Crosby records, Bull Durham, and Milky Way Bars!

War imposes more hardships than meets the eye – and V-MAIL is certainly one of them. It leaves room for little more than facts, and very few of those. But though these letters seem short and pointed, remember that my heart and thoughts are constantly with you and home and all that it holds. Without your love, I would have less strength and less to give. I'm living for the future. Keep the light burning – this won't last forever. Pfc. Lincoln

Imogene:

Tuesday, March 2, 1943

The only excitement at the store today was the 45 minute sale of nylon hose of which I bought 3 pair. Gad! What a mess! You should have seen it! (She worked at the May Company in downtown L. A.)

Wednesday, March 17, 1943

What a St. Patrick's Day to remember! Your first "V" letter arrived today!

Oh, darling, I cannot put into words the thrill of seeing your handwriting again & to have you tell me you love me & to know that you are safe & well. It has put new life into me & now the days won't seem so long. I got stationary today and wrote you my first "V" letter. I'll write every night, now. I love you forever.

V-mail or Victory Mail was a means of letter writing during WWII used to cut down on the cost of transferring mail, and to censor it. After the military post censored the letters, they were copied to film, and then printed back to paper before delivery to the recipient. We have a stack of Link's. The envelopes are 3.8"x4.6" and the single sheet papers are 4.2"x5.1"

Link:

August 1943

Censorship has relaxed to the extent that I may now fill you in on some of the things that you have long been wondering about. We recently left New Zealand, our base since we shipped out from California, and are presently living in what the travel brochures mistakenly refer to as Paradise. We are somewhere in the South Pacific, sheltered by coconut palms and surrounded by scenery that under different circumstances might be considered beautiful. Although to those of us here, the only beautiful spot on earth right now is home.

The character of New Zealand and its people stayed with Link his entire life. The carved Maori god he bought there sat in the living room of every one of their homes. He longed to return, but never made it. That South Pacific Island he refers to at this point is Guadalcanal – the place where the 3rd Marine Division prepared for battle.

We spent our time in New Zealand training and preparing for events to come. That country is a strange little place – the mountains, hills and valleys are so much like our own that it feels like America in miniature. The people are very hospitable and seem resigned to sacrifice, having sent a terrific proportion of their men to war. They like Americans and don't regard themselves as Englishmen – just members of the British Commonwealth. Their stores are quite depleted of stock goods and rations of all types.

The war news is looking better all the time, although war from this vantage point consists of just a lot of hard work. From our tiny locale we can hardly visualize the scope of the entire allied effort. It's too bad the same amount of effort, of any war, couldn't be used to perpetuate life, rather than destroy it. Maybe such a utopia will be reached some day. In the meantime I shall devote all my efforts to creating as great and secure a sanctum for us as work and application permit.

Good night, my darling. I love you with all my heart. Keep the light burning – it can't be forever. Your husband. L.

September 1943

Just three more days and I will have been back in the Marines one year. In some ways it doesn't seem very long, but when I count the time away from you it seems like forever.

*Work is difficult in this climate, and I continue to lose
weight, but not to any degree of danger. I was visualizing you
and Teddy waiting for me at the station when I arrive home,
and he would say, "Look, Mom, isn't that Pop?" And you would
answer, "No dear, remember, Pop was much bigger." Is that as
funny as I think, or is it the heat getting to me? My hair seems
to be changing color, but if you like gray you will be more in love
with me than ever.*

*Teddy's comments in his last letter about this character
Frank Sinatra were great. He just can't figure out why the
young girls are going crazy for some skinny kid from New
Jersey. The boys and I don't really understand it either. We
have a number of "Brooklyns" in our Company and their
language is quite unique. One of them says "ting" instead of
thing, and we tell him that "ting" is what a bell does. Unruffled,
he always responds, "You bums ain't so hot wit Webster eder."*

*We have a young company commander whose a by-the-book
type. He told me he regarded me very highly for my ability to do
my job well and for an alert mind. "However, Corporal Hart,"
he said, "you're about as subtle as a house on fire." On one
occasion I was carrying explosive blasting caps in my pocket.
When he found out, he was horrified and went to great lengths
to explain the danger of such practice. Then in summation, he
asked, "Corporal Hart, what kind of work were you engaged in
on the outside?" "Sir," I replied, "I was an explosives engineer."
With that, he was devoid of any further comment. And so go my
little sorties with a character to whom I'd be hesitant to hire as
a junior clerk at a five and ten.*

My love to all, and keep our light burning. L.xxxxxx

WWII Home front

In addition to housing Marines on leave in Hollywood,
Imogene also decided to do more for the war effort by taking a
job at Lockheed Vega, Burbank. They were manufacturing
military aircraft at the time. Her job was in the Employee
Transportation Department. She was in charge of issuing
ration coupons based on the distance the employees had to
travel to work. With ration coupons of all kinds like gold during
the war, it was an enviable position. Loyal to the core, however,
she never took advantage of it. My father, Ted, said she

wouldn't take one gallon more than was necessary for them. It was a little disappointing for him. He had his driver's license by the age of fourteen – an exception during the War for young people helping support their families while their fathers were away. A normal teenager, he wouldn't have minded a bit of cruising by to see friends on his way to and from his job as a bag boy at Ralph's grocery store.

As children of Hollywood, my parents loved the nights the search lights would light the skies above their homes. It meant yet another movie premiere, with all its glamour and excitement. During the war, those search lights were put to another use, often scanning the darkness for enemy aircraft all night long. Enemy aircraft never appeared.

Ted's most excellent adventure was ignited by the shortage of labor during the War. With so many men gone, there were few left to operate the thousands of farms and ranches spread throughout rural America. One of those was Art and Inge's ranch highlighted in the "Callings" chapter.

With only Art and one ranch hand left to work his 6,000 Wyoming acres, a request was made of my grandmother to send my dad there for the summer of '44. A Los Angeles boy soon found himself trading the wheel of Annabelle, their Model A Ford, for the reins of one of Art's broncos.

Calf-pulling; branding; castrating; moving cattle between pastures; milking the two cows; and harvesting wheat with the Texas combines through the night – he did it all.

And as with those who lived through World War II, both on the battlefield and at home, the experiences wove into the fabric of his being.

THE KOREAN WAR

There was the war into which every man, woman and child in the country put their backs and their hearts. And then there was the war that the country would prefer to ignore. The Korean War. My father's war.

With its start in June of 1950, it was just too close on the heels of World War II for most Americans to stomach. So they didn't talk about it if they could help it. That was a point driven home by my father's story of the unexpected reaction he received upon his return after his service as a Signalman on the U.S.S. *Gregory*, a destroyer. The nickname for destroyers was Tin Cans, because they were small and expendable.

When their assignment in Korea was over, the *Gregory* sailed for San Diego, with a stop in Hawaii. Given liberty, my father and his buddy were at the bar on the beach in front of the Ala Moana – in uniform. A young woman approached them and asked, "Where have you been?"

Where have we been? They wondered at her ignorance. "There's a war going on just across that ocean. Haven't you heard?"

When he got back to California, the same question came up again and again from people who'd just figured out he'd been missing for the last two years. "Where have you been?" they'd ask.

"In North Korea. Plucking downed pilots out of Wonsan Harbor," he'd answer. "There's a war going on. Perhaps you haven't heard."

While folks back home concentrated on sending wives back to the kitchen and men to the office or factories, 33,686 Americans lost their lives fighting in that three-year war that no one wanted to talk about; with 4,759 missing in action.

On their return home, the *Gregory* sailed into Pearl Harbor, where the Navy band and Hula dancers greeted them. The *Arizona* had not been made a monument at that time. It was just resting there as it had been since December 7, 1941. Sailors often took the time to motor over to the sunken ship. It was possible to walk on the deck that was still visible just above the water line. Ted had done that on his minority cruise in 1948. He didn't climb aboard on that second trip. When I asked him why, it was hard for him to even get the words out.

THE VIETNAM WAR

Johnny (1950–2004) Maternal second cousin. Staff Sergeant, United States Army, Company B, 2nd Battalion (Airmobile), 5th Cavalry

As a teacher of American literature, I ended each school year with a unit on the Vietnam War and the novel *The Things They Carried* by Tim O'Brien. In June of 1999, I decided I could no longer put off speaking with the source of so many of my own memories of that strange and turbulent period – my cousin Johnny.

My mother tracked down his phone number for me, and I dialed it with apprehension. Would he want to talk with me about those things that most veterans locked away in the corner of their minds decades ago? Would he remember the letters of a silly seventeen year old, much more preoccupied with proms than POWs?

When I heard his voice, all my worries melted away. It reminded me that Johnny was a sweet and easy-going guy. After the usual niceties, I got down to the reason for my call.

"The last memory I have of you during the Vietnam War is the visit my mom, brother, and I made to the hospital at Fort Ord after you were wounded," I said, searching for a way to begin. "The image that I carry is of a cavernous room lined with perfectly spaced beds mounded with wounded men. My other memories of the fort are of a blur of khaki green uniforms on the firing ranges by the dunes, and a very long line of soldiers in white t-shirts, sleeves rolled up and blood dripping down both arms from the vaccinations they'd just received. But I guess that's the end of the story for you. If you're willing, I'd like to hear the whole thing – from the beginning."

"The whole thing, huh? It's not that interesting."

"Sure it is. I've been reading one of your letters from Vietnam and talking about you to my students for five years. It's only fair that I share your story from your point of view."

Johnny began his hour-long tale of bureaucracy and bravery.

"In 1968, I had been out of high school for awhile and hadn't really made any long-range plans for my life, so I decided to enlist. Most of my friends were being drafted anyway. As an infantryman in the First Cavalry Division, my tour of duty was two years. It was inevitable that I'd be sent to Vietnam. So, when I found out that officers spent six months in the field and six months in the rear, I decided that it sounded a lot safer to be an officer. My training took place in Fort Ord, California, and Fort Benning, Georgia.

"Day one in Vietnam, I was inserted into a firebase that was being mortared by overlapping cannon fire. By day two, I was declared the man in charge. I had just gotten there; didn't know anybody; and I was the one who was supposed to be giving orders. The guys taking the orders weren't too impressed.

"Day three, we were inserted into a bunker complex that was a half-mile wide and a mile long. Bunker complexes kind of remind me of ant farms – *that* busy and *that* crowded. Anyway, we were immediately pinned down for three days. Three days without the ability to even stick our heads up out of that bunker! Welcome to Vietnam!

"Most of my memories of my time in the field run together. You know, soldiers are trained to do exactly as they're told – which is sometimes a good way to get killed. I'm a pretty calm guy, with just plain common sense, and my men trusted me.

"We moved during the day. It was guerilla warfare, you know. There was no way the Americans were going to win. We just weren't trained for it. But *they were*. The fighting took place at night. We'd set up in a circle with the radio and heavy artillery in the middle. Most of the time we were attacking the wood line. You rarely saw what was behind that line. If we got into trouble on the ground, we'd radio for fire support, which came by air.

"So the days went like this. We would receive orders by radio to march to a particular set of coordinates, because VC or NVA activity had been spotted in that area. We'd march single file, watching for snipers in the wood line. By dark, we had set up in our circle. If the enemy engaged us, we'd try to deal with them ourselves. If we couldn't, we'd call for air support."

I knew that Johnny had earned several medals, including the Army Commendation Medal for Heroism, so I asked, "Would you mind talking about the battle in which you were wounded?"

"Well, you know, by 1970 they weren't sending any new troops to Vietnam, and we weren't supposed to have any troops in Cambodia. So, anyway, in June of that year my company was fighting pretty close to the Cambodian border. Then this one day, our company commander tells us that we're going to be inserted by helicopter twenty-six miles *inside* Cambodia.

"My men and I knew that was insane. There was no fire support for us over there if we got into trouble. And we knew there had been a lot of NVA activity in that area. So my platoon and I talked it over and decided I'd approach the commander and inform him of the error of his ways. I did just that, basically telling him that the mission was suicidal, and we weren't going. He naturally told me that if we *didn't* go we'd be court marshaled for mutiny. And because I dared talk to him, I and my platoon were not only going, but we had moved to the head of the list.

"A few hours later, the Company was twenty-six miles inside the Cambodian border. That first night, we set up in concentric rings, with the commanding officers and rockets in the center of the ring. We were ambushed at four that morning – taking a hit directly into the center of our circle. Every one of the officers was either killed or wounded. That left two staff sergeants as the highest ranking officers in the company. I was one of them. I was now the new company commander.

"After evacuating the bodies and wounded by air, we were radioed our orders. That day, as I was leading a ten-man squad down a trail, I happened to look to my right and noticed two guys in green uniforms standing on a path that dissected the trail. It's just like they tell you… Time seemed to move in slow motion. The men were backlit. As I stared at them, I realized something wasn't exactly right. It was their guns. They were AK47s – the guns that the enemy carried. I called for my men to hit the dirt, pulled out a grenade and tossed it in their direction. It didn't go off. In the meantime, they also hit the dirt. I was on a berm, which placed me just high enough above them for my first shots to go over their heads. Just as I was about to readjust my sites, they launched a grenade that exploded two feet from me. I ended up with thirteen holes in my body – on my chin, hairline, right side, and left hand. It also punctured my eardrums."

"I remember when they called your mother about you, all they said was that you had been wounded," I said. "The family didn't know where you were for a couple of days."

"That's right. I was flown to Tokyo first; then on to Fort Ord to recover."

"Your records don't say anything about your being in Cambodia."

"According to our government, we weren't there."

"How did you come through Vietnam without the serious mental ailments that many vets experience?"

"There was an expression that I and my buddies used whenever anything happened – good or bad. *It don't mean nothin.* It was a way of not caring enough about anything or anyone, so you'd never be hurt. It was the way we – I – survived."

"That's so sad."

"Sad – but necessary. You just couldn't trust anyone but yourself. I remember one of the times when we were in the rear, every morning for what seemed like weeks, we'd wake up to find that one of the men had been shot by a sniper. Here we were, supposedly removed from the fighting, and we were being systematically eliminated. Turns out it was the *sweet* little man who picked up and delivered the laundry every morning. He was VC. Yeah. *It didn't mean nothin.*"

After I hung up the phone, I mentally traced through the spring of 1970, my last semester of high school. The first Earth Day. Burying a car at San Jose State to protest who knows what. Senior Ball. Altamont. The Beatles breaking up. The Black Panther movement. Cheering at basketball games. What an incongruent mix of events. Then as I shuffled through the papers Johnny sent me, I noticed the date he was wounded – June 12th – my graduation day. So, while I was sitting in the sunshine on the football field, surrounded by friends and family, optimistic about the glorious life waiting for me, my cousin was clinging to life in a helicopter hundreds of feet above a war and a country for which he had little loyalty or understanding.

The assassinations and body counts – were they so much a part of our everyday lives that we became immune to the true horror of the events? Or, was it a case of out of sight, out of mind? Can people really be that self-centered?

Through the hundreds of interviews about the Vietnam era written by my students, I came to realize that the gap of understanding was so wide – generation to generation; grunt to commander; politician to constituent; soldier to war protester; blue collar to white collar, that it has yet to be bridged.

And so the legacy lives on in distrust of the government; distrust of the young; distrust of the other.

Yes. People really can be that self-centered.

At the time I wrote the above, I had no idea that Johnny's suffering hadn't ended on the battlefield. He had terrible nightmares at first. And he squeezed bits of shrapnel out of his body for years. At the age of fifty-four, he was diagnosed with cancer and died a short while later. Was it the result of exposure to Agent Orange while in Vietnam? Hard to say. But when he departed – far too young – he left his family and our world with one less really good guy and one less quiet hero.

Here are the words from the Department of the Army regarding his Commendation Medal. June 14, 1970:

For heroism in connection with military operations against a hostile force in the Republic of Vietnam. Staff Sergeant Atkins distinguished himself by valorous action on 12 June 1970. Becoming engaged with a determined enemy force, he displayed great courage and determination in his efforts to neutralize the enemy threat. With complete disregard for his own safety, he exposed himself to the danger inherent in the combat environment, and even after being wounded, continued to exert every effort to defeat the hostiles. His heroic and valiant actions were characterized by a great concern for the welfare of his comrades and contributed materially to the successful accomplishment of the United States mission in the Republic of Vietnam. His loyalty, diligence, and devotion to duty are in keeping with the highest traditions of the military service and reflect utmost credit upon himself, his unit, and the United States Army.

Successful accomplishment of the United States Mission in the Republic of Vietnam. We all know how that ended. Much like the Korean War. Except with a peace treaty. The recorded military deaths are 58,318 killed in action or non-combat deaths (including the missing and deaths in captivity) – 1,589 missing in action (originally 2,426). That doesn't include the thousands of soldiers who were exposed to Agent Orange and later died and continue to die of various cancers.

With the Vietnam War a devastating foregone conclusion, it's understandable why Johnny and his men shielded themselves with a *It don't mean nothin* attitude.

After spending hours and hours ensconced in the war stories of my family members, however, I have to respectfully disagree. Your service did mean something, Johnny. As did the service of Leonard, Benjamin, Hewlett, Jacob, Harry, Lee, Link, Ted and all the rest. You forged the United States of America and then fought to keep America united. You bested the most evil fascists the world has ever known. You rushed in to defend the oppressed all over the globe. And despite arrogant and ill-guided commanders, you stepped up and performed your duty. You, the little guys, the Marines, soldiers and sailors, you put your very lives on the line. You are the brave, who make it possible for the rest of us to rest our heads in the land of the free. And for that, we give our eternal thanks.

6

TRAILBLAZERS, VISIONARIES & PEACEMAKERS

As explained below in the introduction to this chapter, most of these ancestors came from the same era. Tying your ancestors to an era is another way to come up with inspirations for your stories. Was your grandmother a Roaring Twenties flapper? Was your mother a 1960s hippie? Did your great-great-grandfather work in a factory during the Industrial Revolution. Did you have ancestors who rode west on a wagon train? Do you have family members who helped build the Transcontinental Railroad; or who lived through the tough times in Europe or Japan immediately after WWII? These all make great stories.

I found information for a few of these stories through used books on Amazon, newspaper articles, and on Wikipedia. I cover more of this in the "Resources" chapter.

I was fortunate to have so much information on these ancestors that the stories are quite complete. For the purposes of this book, I only include short summaries of the stories to give you the idea of how they fit into the chapter theme.

In a way, all my ancestors were trailblazers. In a westward-leading, serpentine line – step-by-step – through outside forces or inner strength, they turned their backs on the familiar and carved lives out of the unknown.

The ancestors in this chapter not only blazed trails with their feet – they did so with their imaginations, curiosity, and intellect. They followed an innate desire for truth and fairness. Their enthusiasm and inspiration gave rise to discoveries and ideas that benefited not only themselves but a broad swath of humanity.

I couldn't help but notice as I reviewed my choice of ancestors, they all lived and thrived in the late 1800s and early 1900s. What was it about that time period, I began to wonder. They certainly weren't alone. The Wright brothers, George Washington Carver, Sigmund Freud, Marie Curie, and somewhat earlier, Charles Darwin, led revolutions in science, engineering, and psychology. Was it the industrial revolution that freed people to use their brains in addition to their brawn? Certainly there were other periods in history that were culturally significant. The thinkers and trailblazers of those times, however, were limited to a small and exceptional group. In the United States at the end of the 19th century, intellectual opportunity had a much broader reach.

Whatever the reason, that period produced an inspiring bunch of folks – who opened the way for others to follow.

Harry B (1875-1921) Paternal great-grandfather

Genetics is a lot more than a predisposition to sticky ear wax. It's at least partly responsible for successive generations of family becoming educators, carpenters, or actors. It's the reason that not only am I a writer, but I like to write both fiction and non-fiction, and on a broad range of subjects. I just found that out.

My great-grandfather is a famous family figure. You tend to be that when you live life large and then die tragically at the age of forty-six. He's also famous because the force was strong in him. His genes are evident in many of his descendants: in auburn hair, the cut of a jaw, the narrowness of shoulder, and a long lanky frame – in an insatiable curiosity; and in a passion for politics, history, literature, and service.

As a young man, he was a newspaper reporter and magazine writer. Entirely self-educated, he passed the Colorado State Bar in 1899 and began practicing law. So highly respected was he that he was appointed to District Attorney for the State of Colorado in 1914. He served in that capacity until he passed away from Spanish influenza on New Year's Day 1921.

Our favorite quote about my great-grandfather comes from a newspaper article about a trial in which he served as the lead prosecutor: "The lean and capable United States District Attorney, who had narrowly escaped being mobbed by the reservation Utes during the course of his personal investigation, presented the government's case."

Lean and capable – we love that. He lost the government's case, by the way, but I somehow think that was okay with him. He certainly wouldn't have wanted to be responsible for starting an Indian war. He was just doing his job.

Referring back to the genetics thing... Even if he were only fifty percent the man represented in the testimonials written after his death, I like to think that some of the best of ourselves can be traced back to lean and capable Harry B.

The Reverend Julia Amanda Deyo (1838-1917)
Sister of my maternal 3rd-great-grandfather

The source for my information on Amanda is an article from *The Hudson Valley Regional Review*, March 1991, Volume 8, Number 1, by William P. McDermott. Amanda also has a Wikipedia page, but the former is so thorough, I relied almost entirely on it. Its subtitle is *A Chrononarrative of a Preacher of Peace*.

And *that* she was:

Raised a Quaker, Amanda became a Universalist minister, with "a firm conviction that peace was an inextricable part of religion. Wishing to spread her beliefs, and aware of her unusually effective abilities to persuade, the Dutchess County, New York native spoke with zeal, in public venues across the country and overseas, about her thoughts and values, and about the need to have a firm conviction about their validity and goodness. Those thoughts included beliefs in women's rights and interests, proper education, especially of children, and temperance."

Amanda and her husband became active members in the New York Peace Society, a branch of the Philadelphia based Universal Peace Union. "While the general theme of the meetings was peace, so often were the issues of temperance, women's rights, children's needs, the plight of minorities, particularly Indians, and other social themes that an unknowing visitor would have concluded the annual meeting was more a general reform movement."

In 1888, she "represented the Universal Peace Union at the annual meeting of the International Council of Women. There, she was in the company of a number of prominent women including Clara Barton, Frances Willard, Julia Ward Howe, Marguerite Moore of Ireland, and Princess Verogna, a Mohawk Indian, all of whom addressed the Council. Princess Verogna chastised the audience for having taught the Indians to use 'alcoholic liquors' and 'to use God's name in vain.'

"The highlight of that year came at the very end. Amanda was appointed to represent the Universal Peace Union at the Universal Peace Congress to be held during the Paris Exposition in June 1889.

"In July 1892, the famous Homestead Riot and Carnegie Steel Mills drew Amanda into a very heated and sometimes bloody dispute between employer and employees. She was appointed (by the Universal Peace Union) to present herself to both sides in the capacity of arbitrator."

After her husband died, in her later years, Amanda moved to the Shaker community in New Lebanon, N.Y. In the Universal Union Papers, Swarthmore College Peace Collection, there is a wonderful photo of her standing with eight Shaker women of all ages.

Dr. William Stewart Halsted (1852-1922) Descendant of the brother of my maternal 8th great-grandparents

All of the information about William Halsted is taken from a biography written by Gerald Imber, MD, entitled *Genius on the Edge: The Bizarre Double Life of Dr. William Stewart Halsted.*

To best understand how important Dr. Halsted was to modern medicine, one only need to read the Afterword in Imber's book:

"William Halsted's death was mourned throughout the surgical world. He was memorialized in a laudatory tribute in the *Baltimore Sun*, in which H.L. Mencken recognized his contributions and contradictions, his icy countenance and his humanity, what he had done to modernize surgery and how he stood out among the great men of (Johns) Hopkins.

"The American public was generally unaware of William Stewart Halsted. He didn't make speeches or befriend the powerful, and the fruit of his seminal work would not fully ripen for at least a generation. At the outset of Halsted's career, fewer than a dozen doctors restricted their practices to the unsustainable, barbaric, and off-putting practice of surgery. Over his 33 years at the helm of surgery at Johns Hopkins, Halsted not only invented an entire surgical philosophy, he instituted a system to inculcate in surgeons this philosophy, which spawned several generations of the finest teachers of surgery in the world.

"His goal was to train 'not only surgeons but surgeons of the highest type, men who will stimulate the first youth of our country to devote their energies and their lives to raising the standards of surgical science.' In this, his success is everywhere to be seen. Of Halsted's 17 residents, 12 became professors of surgery, associate professors, assistant professors, or surgeons in chief. Forty-six of his 55 assistant residents held academic titles, and the residents of his residents came to lead major surgical faculties throughout the country.

"Virtually every academically affiliated surgeon can trace his or her teachers, and teacher's teachers, to William Stewart Halsted.

"Far more impressive is the fact that every well-trained surgeon is trained in a Halsted-type system, and all still live by the Halsted principles of surgery. Aseptic technique, gentle handling of tissue, scrupulous hemostasis, and tension-free, crush-free, and anatomically proper surgery are the rules. And they are Halsted rules. Although "Halsted" is not a household name, every individual in America who undergoes successful surgery owes William Stewart Halsted a nod and a deep debt of gratitude."

The rest of the details of Dr. Halsted's life fills a book!

Dr. Margaretta (Aunt Margaret) (1876-1953)
Paternal great-great-aunt

Dr. Halsted's biography is over 350 pages. There is no biography of Dr. Margaretta. In fact, it took a lot of detective work to even piece her life together. The first thing I remember hearing about her was that she delivered my dad, all ten pounds of him, at the family home in Denver. And then there were her steamer trunks, ever-present in my parent's garage and filled with all sorts of oddities: photographs; bound copies of *Harper's Weekly*; campaign and bicycle buttons; souvenir programs; a tiny copy of the *Common Book of Prayer*; marbles; an acorn – all from the late 1800s. Carefully recorded in her small script, Aunt Margaret included information on the items in letters and on lists.

Aunt Margaret herself was a gem – a gem without heirs. And that, we believe, is the other reason that in the waning years of her life she sent her precious belongings to my parents. I'm glad she did, too, because they are a conduit to her. And they allow me the privilege of making sure she's not forgotten.

Aunt Margaret and her siblings were raised in Pittsburgh, Pennsylvania. Her father died when she was only nine. One of her two brothers died on his twenty-second birthday when she was fifteen. It must have been two of the factors that created such a close bond between Aunt Margaret, her mother, and her surviving brother.

According to a letter Aunt Margaret wrote to my parents, she graduated with honors from Gross Medical College in Denver in April 1899. I researched the percentage of women to men in the medical profession during that period and found that it was only around five percent.

As we learned from William Stewart Halsted's story, right about the time he and his fellow doctors were revolutionizing the profession was when Aunt Margaret threw her stethoscope into the ring. According to my father, she was quite small of stature and proper of bearing. From her photographs, she definitely looks the tiny but mighty type. She would have to be to garner any respect and earn the trust of patients.

According to her obituary, after an internship, she began practice in Denver and later set up practice in Colorado Springs. Also according to her obituary, Aunt Margaret went to

New York for post-graduate work and also studied in Berlin, Vienna, and London. When she returned to the U.S. she became head physician at Maternity Hospital in Minneapolis for two years. She re-established her practice in Denver after that.

Aunt Margaret never married, but I'm guessing her medical practice kept her fulfilled. She may not have had children of her own, but she had all those patients to nurture. I can just see her making house calls, carrying the traditional black bag, and carrying herself with confidence.

I doubt whether Aunt Margaret thought of herself as a trailblazer. But she certainly was. In pursuing a career in medicine she chose a different path from most of her contemporaries. It must have taken a lot of courage to take part in surgery rounds with most of the other residents being men. William Stewart Halsted had only referenced men when speaking of attracting qualified young minds to the profession. I'm quite certain she would have met Dr. Halsted's qualifications. When my grandmother spoke of her rough labor and delivery of my father, she always attributed her getting through it without after-effects to Aunt Margaret.

And my grandmother was just one of thousands of patients she helped in her fifty-plus year career. I do hope in the end that it had been a good life for Aunt Margaret. She deserved it.

To Where the Sun Sets

7

VILLAINS & BLACKSHEEP

I hope you are fortunate enough to have a few ancestors who fit into a chapter of this title. They really do make for great stories. They tend to be the type of stories that you may have heard rather than read, and more than once. Infamy makes a great headliner for dinner table chats.

The Moravians and Society of Friends (Quakers) kept great records. The lives of my black sheep Charles, Jane Cox, and Sarah Cox were uncovered through these records. How to access them is included in the "Resources" chapter.

If I asked my sons what TV show from their childhood had the greatest impact on their thinking about what makes people tick, I believe they'd say, *Joseph Campbell and The Power of Myth.* It was a PBS series that aired in 1988, six one-hour conversations between Bill Moyer and Joseph Campbell. We even had the series on tape and listened to it while commuting to school. I'm sure part of the attraction was that the references Campbell uses to illustrate his thoughts are often from the *Star Wars* series – the gold standard in movies around our household.

According to the Bill Moyer website, the idea of the series was "to explore what enduring myths can tell us about our lives... Moyers and Campbell focus on a character or theme found in cultural and religious mythologies. Campbell argues that these timeless archetypes continue to have a powerful influence on the choices we make and the ways we live."

As a literature teacher, I incorporated Joseph Campbell's *Hero's Journey* when exploring the plots and characters of any number of stories, from ancient to modern. Given the opportunity, I could apply that circular pattern to the lives of most real folks, as well. For everything between birth and death is pretty much a hero's journey. As the protagonist of our own story, we get the call; cross the threshold into new experience; find a mentor and a friend or two to help along the way; bounce through our road of trials; challenge our antagonists; change; grow; earn our freedom; and return to tell our tale.

This chapter focuses on antagonists, some of the most compelling characters on the hero's journey. All really good plots require them. Overcoming them is the way ordinary humans grow and change, become extraordinary – sometimes even heroes.

We'll start with Villains – which may be a little harsh, as I never met these people. There are two sides to every story, after all. Perhaps, like Darth Vader, they had their reasons and finally found redemption.

Carlotta (c.1850-?) Maternal great-great-grandmother's sister

The atrocities Carlotta inflicted on Maria are covered in the "Callings" chapter. Maria's response to them were no less than heroic. Carlotta does not seem to have acquired a conscience at any point in her life. Long after Maria left Germany, Carlotta continued her evil, conniving ways. After Maria and family moved to the Los Angeles area, Carlotta made sure to acquire the contact information for Maria's children and grandchildren. Over the years, she succeeded in convincing some of them that members of her family in Germany were hungry, destitute, and in need of money. My Aunt Jean was one who was taken in. She sent money to the German contingent over the years. And then while on a European vacation, Jean decided to stop in and meet that part of the family. They were living in a large lovely home, with a well-stocked larder. No surprise there!

Virginia (c.1851-?) Maternal great-great-grandmother

Virginia's parents were the ancestors who owned the Moore House, mentioned in the "War Stories" chapter. Her husband was Eugene, also mentioned. Virginia's is one of those stories so odd, mysterious, and unbelievable it has become family legend.

Eugene and Virginia had four children. The oldest was my great-grandfather (Grandad), followed by two brothers and a sister. A graduate of the engineering department of the College of William and Mary, Eugene was in Maui in 1886, helping construct the government road around the island. Virginia was living in Baltimore with the children – perhaps with her parents, at their home.

When Grandad was twelve, Virginia gathered up all her children and took them to the train station. Leaving them on a bench, she went off to buy the tickets, or so the children thought. Minutes passed and then more, without any sign of their mother. When finally so much time had gone by that Grandad knew something was very wrong, he led his siblings out of the station and to his grandparents.

Legend has it that Virginia had taken off with a circus performer – a perfect plot twist for this story! And if that circus travelled by train, it fits. Whether anyone ever went back to the station to ask if she had purchased a ticket or been seen, I don't know.

I assume that Eugene was contacted, but mail delivery between Baltimore and Maui had to have taken quite a while.

In the meantime, Grandad's five-year-old sister, Marie, was sent to live with a cousin in Poughkeepsie, New York. I don't know where his seven-year-old brother Joseph ended up, until three years later in Hollywood with Eugene. His ten-year-old brother Otis was sent to live with and was adopted by a family in San Diego. Grandad was put on a sailing ship and made a cabin boy.

The fallout from dividing those siblings stretched across generations. Marie remained in New York, never rejoining her father or brothers. Otis was very bitter, and refused to have anything to do with his father and siblings for years.

A final mystery about Virginia: One day in the early 1900s, when Grandad was working at the Fremont Hotel in downtown

Los Angeles, the front desk clerk told him that there was a woman with his mother's name registered as a guest. He called her room. It was his mother! He asked if he could come up and see her. At the appointed time, he knocked on her door. No answer. She was gone! That was the last trace anyone ever had of her.

There are two conclusions we can draw from this: since she was still using Eugene's last name, she hadn't married that circus performer. And, she was ruled by fear or pride, or both.

On to Black Sheep – distinguishable from villains by their likeability. Also, though some of them can be antagonistic, it is often the antagonists in their own lives that motivated them to flee the flock.

Although generations apart, the following two women from the same family were condemned for the same religious reason. At that period, Quakers were as intolerant as Puritans when it came to matters of the heart:

Sarah Cox Leech (1690-1755)
Paternal 7th great-grandmother
"Was complained of to Kennett (Pennsylvania) Monthly Meeting 12 June 1712 'for marrying contrary to her parents' and friends' minds.'"

Jane Leech(1768-1854) Paternal 4th great-grandmother and great-granddaughter of Sarah Cox Leech
On 8 August 1786 and 11 November 1786, Jane was complained of at the Warrington, York County, Pennsylvania Meeting for marriage to one not a member. The case was submitted to a committee on 13 January 1787, and 10 March 1787 "she is removed a considerable distance." On 7 April 1787 she was disbound."

Charles Holder (1744-1808)
Maternal 5th great-grandfather
This is small sample of the life of Charles, taken from the records of the Moravian Church at Wachovia (now Old Salem) and differs somewhat from the genealogical account, which describes Charles as a very holy man. A separate record was kept on every individual, and the entries given to Charles

Holder were more voluminous than most; maybe his was the most of all.

His sins:

Of the more than 175 entries for Charles in the Moravian records, dating from November 1766 to his death in February 1808, at least sixty of them concern his debts and his work habits, or lack thereof.

The first one is dated 22 May 1772: "Charles Holder wants to buy his house. It is a great question, however, if it would be good for him and for us... because he does not conduct his business so that he could really spare something; from which many troubles come and about which we should talk to him."

If they only knew... They would have done more than just talk to him.

The last is dated 16 February 1808, eleven days after his death: "It is reported that Charles Bagge, as executor of Charles Holder's estate, is willing to pay for the debts of his father-in-law."

In between, there were entries, such as:

1772 "There may be more debts about which we do not know anything certain. We believe this is the consequence of his lazy and easy-going way of life, to which we have given him too free a hand by showing him that he is useful for different things such as doing errands, measuring lands, slaughtering... As he got payment for this work, he led a lazy life days after working, and we are afraid that at such occupations he gets too much used to strong drink."

1776 "It was mentioned hereby that with Charles it is always the same old way of life. He does not like to work, otherwise he could get along very well... It would be much better for him if he, when he has run short of work, tries to get some kind of day labor than hang around in the town and do nothing but try to arouse the pity of the citizens. It was also mentioned that his wife should rather stay at home and not run around the town all the time. That she should better try to take care of the household." *Yes. His wife, Johanna, too!*

10 November 1789 "Br. Charles was rather embarrassed through the suggestion to have another saddler come here..." (Saddler was Charles' occupation.)

Apparently not embarrassed enough to change his ways,

because...

18 November 1795 "Certain trades are entirely wanting here and others are poorly manned, as e.g., the saddlery."

I told you they were patient. And really poor judges of a man's abilities. When it came time to pick a new night watchman, who did they choose? Charles.

4 February 1785 "Br. Holder has accepted to take over the night watch for a certain time."

19 April 1785 "There are again complaints that Charles Holder does not take care of the night watch as he should."

27 September 1785 "Last night two horses were stolen out of the tavern stable..."

13 October 1785 "Quite recently a number of horses have been stolen in and around Salem... In this connection it was reported that in spite of his promises to improve his punctuality, etc., the night watchman has completely lost the confidence of the community."

And yet... 10 August 1786 "Many horses were stolen in our neighborhood recently..."

Did they not see this coming?!

Before we leave Charles, some things in his favor:

He was the only one in the village who knew how to sweep a chimney.

He made the leather fire buckets for the community, an important safeguard. My parents saw one that Charles made when they visited Old Salem.

He was one of the leading town musicians. Although...

13 June 1781 "Br. Holder must give up trombone-blowing on account of physical weakness."

And finally, for Charles, there was still hope...

5 February 1808 "The last day of his life, he was still heard earnestly praying, "My Jesus – my dearest Saviour – have mercy upon me; receive me as a poor sinner, who has nothing at all to show by thy merit.' And after that he said, 'Oh, how wonderful! My whole soul rejoices that I am already included with the number of the redeemed.'"

*You have to love him - **for** his flaws - **not** in spite of them. For the Charles in all of us.*

8

THE GOLDEN STATE

My final chapter includes the stories of relatives closest to me in generation. I suggest you end your history this way as well. These are the stories you either heard or witnessed yourself. These are the stories that, if you're lucky, you can collect by talking to your mother, uncle, or older sibling. These stories are family lore. If you choose, this is the perfect place for you to include your own story.

As you can see, I decided to use place as a theme. That was because in my family most ancestral paths led to Southern California. A character unto itself, it played greatly into their lives. You may also have a place where many family members ended up – a place that helps define your spirit. If so, use that as your theme. If not – if your family ended up in several different areas – you could use a trait or two that defines your collective "who" – persistence, courage, humor... Or, use chronology, starting either with your great-grandparents and working forward, or you and working back.

You will notice I incorporate quite a few news articles, obituaries, speeches, travel journals, eulogies, because I didn't have to dig back as far for this section.

I also incorporate a lot of detail – soft-boiled eggs, piccolos, and the family parrot. Don't think of these things as trivial. They are

*the frosting on the cake that is their lives. They are the stories
that my grandchildren ask me to repeat over and over and over
– making sure I leave nothing out.*

These are the stories, my friends, that you need to collect **now**,
while there are still people who can fill in blanks.
These are the stories that give you the opportunity to connect.
These are the stories that will save your lives.

WHO WOULDN'T WANT TO LIVE IN HOLLYWOOD?

Those are the words of my father, echoing from the orange
blossom and gardenia scented memories of his youth. My
mother, born and raised in Hollywood, shares the same idyllic
view.

Magic.

That's what the place was. Pure magic.

Sunshine. A hint of the sea carried on a westerly breeze.
Searchlights guiding the way to Grauman's Chinese Theatre.
Movie stars jumping right off the screen and onto the sidewalk
in front of your bungalow. The Red Cars carrying you from
Santa Monica to Glendale to downtown Los Angeles to
Huntington Beach, if you chose to venture that far. Your
parents never worrying about where you were. Or, about
getting you from place to place. That was your job. You had two
good legs. If you were lucky, a bike. And, as you got older, the
family car. And also as you got older, one of countless jobs in an
economy that took off in the 1880s and never looked back. For
my grandparents' generation, they could always find work at
one of the studios. The teens and twenties were the age of films
with casts of a thousand.

And none of this was any secret. Entrepreneurial types took
one look at the place and knew they had discovered the second
California gold rush. The first ad campaign was the fruit crates
sent by trains all over the USA, with artwork depicting a
paradise for the picking. Word of mouth didn't hurt. Letters
sent home extolling the place. The movie industry with its
universal appeal, and opportunities for employment at places
where the magic happened cemented the deal.

By my childhood, there was what I call the Pasadena Rose

Parade effect. It's New Year's Day. You're sitting in your den in Massachusetts or Iowa, shivering under your sweaters and blankets, casting your eyes to the leaden skies outside your window. When your eyes shift back to your brand new color television set, there before you drift white puffy clouds on a crystal blue sky. Below it people in shirt sleeves cheer at flower-covered floats and jaunty marching bands. "Mabel! Get in here! The announcer just said it's eighty degrees there. Eighty!" And Los Angeles adds ten thousand more citizens to its tax rolls by Spring.

It's no wonder the population of the city of L.A. exploded from eleven thousand in 1880 to two and a half million by 1960. The Rose Parade effect still kicks in every New Year's Day, by the way. The population as of 2019 is four million and counting.

My family members were among the earlier arrivals – coming in ones or twos, or sometimes the whole gang. And what a life they had. I don't think there was a one who wouldn't have agreed with my father.

Eugene (1851-1928) Maternal great-great grandfather

You will recall that Eugene was the ancestor who received his engineering degree from the College of William and Mary; managed Temple Farm in Yorktown, Virginia; supervised the construction of the government road circling the island of Maui; and whose wife, Virginia, left their kids at the Baltimore train station during the period Eugene was in Maui.

We believe that on Eugene's way to Maui, he must have stopped in Southern California, and perhaps then began dreaming of building a life there. On his return voyage in 1889, he disembarked and never went back to the East.

When Eugene got to Hollywood, which at the time was called Prospect, he immediately jumped into development, buying lots and building bungalows. He built his own iconic large-scale bungalow and carriage house on an acre of land at Hollywood Boulevard and Vista Street in 1904. At that time, the boulevard was still called Prospect Avenue and was a dirt road. According to Wikipedia, the city name change occurred in 1910, when Hollywood voted to merge with Los Angeles in order to secure an adequate water supply and to gain access to the L.A. sewer system. Eugene planted the first palm trees along the boulevard.

From the wide and deep porches of their home, Eugene and his second wife, Rebecca, watched over the city that they helped grow from the ground up. They were accompanied by their parrot, Polly, who lived to be over a hundred years old.

When the debate ensued over whether to widen Hollywood Boulevard Eugene argued that it would be entirely unnecessary, as it was wide enough for two hay carts to pass. They were also opposed to the commercial buildings and apartments which were starting to pop up. They didn't want the beauty and serenity of their neighborhood disturbed. Their souls would weep if they stood today on the busy intersection of Hollywood and Vista, completely surrounded by apartments.

I'd rather think of them as they were remembered by their fellow Hollywood citizens – Eugene in his wide white sombrero at the reins of a team of large white horses, guiding his runabout down Hollywood Boulevard with Rebecca at his side. There is a photograph of Eugene in that sombrero hanging on my wall. It's a classic, as was he. I also have a photograph of Rebecca, with my grandmother, great-grandmother and great-aunt in the runabout posed on Hollywood Boulevard. In the background – nothing but orchards.

William (Grandad) (1874-1965) Maternal great-grandfather

I'm not sure if being abandoned by his father and mother defined Grandad. But it did set him off on an adventure that's the stuff of little boys' dreams. Why someone thought it was a good idea for a twelve-year-old to leave school and sail around the world for two years as a cabin boy, I have no idea. But, that he did.

I'm pretty sure Grandad would have been a storyteller no matter how his life unfolded. But his family, or anyone who happened to join him on his front porch for that matter, had their imaginations fired by stories so rich they were forever grateful to his having completed his hero's journey within their reach.

Almost all the following about Grandad is from primary source material from his descendants. When the subject of Grandad comes up, invariably we talk about his stories;

compare notes; fill in gaps for each other. We also agree that he was not above embellishment for dramatic effect. I would say, then, that you can take most of this to be true. Most...

For Grandad, I think I'll start at the end. He died at the age of ninety-two. And the first time he ever went to a doctor was a couple years before that. To what do we attribute his longevity? A total lack of stress, for starters. The man was completely content rocking on a swing, swatting flies, and studying his giant thermometer. Or puttering in his garage. Or donning his pith helmet and knocking avocados out of the tree in his backyard with a giant stick. I accompanied him on all of these activities. And they were delightful.

Mostly, though, he spent his time in the shade of his front porch, feeding blue jays from his open palm and watching the neighbors stroll by. Before my time, Polly the parrot, who he inherited from his father, was on the porch with him. When a woman walked by, Polly would let out a loud wolf whistle. The woman would stop and look up at Grandad, wondering what the old man was about. He'd just sit there, a gleam in his eye, the corners of his mouth turned up under his thick gray mustache.

So, no stress. And a simple diet. He ate toast and a soft boiled egg every morning. I can see that egg even now resting in a white egg cup on a stand. He'd tap it with the back of his spoon until it cracked. Peel away the shell. Shake salt and pepper on it. Then slowly make his way down to the bottom. Why was that so fascinating to me?

Then there was his nightly sherry. Only one sherry-glass full. Or rather, that's what he brought out of the kitchen to enjoy in the living room. Funny how he'd disappear into the kitchen on and off for the rest of the evening...

The only workout he ever got was walking at a leisurely pace. And, again, he lived to be ninety-two.

Now, you might think that these activities were confined to Grandad's golden years. In actuality, all of Grandad's years were golden. My father and mother figure he left his last regular job when he was in his fifties. That was "locksmith to the stars" at the hardware store at Gardner Junction. I was told he'd come home with stories about making keys for the rich and famous. His job before that was at Hollywood Auto

Top Shop, replacing and repairing cloth tops on cars. There couldn't have been much call for that beyond the 1920s. My mother has the tool he used to repair the tops.

Even when he was working, he never did so in the summer. For decades, he would pack up the tents, cook stove, gear – oh, and his wife, Bam, and head for the High Sierras. In a pretty little spot along Sherwin Creek, he'd construct an elaborate campsite with all the comforts of home. And there they'd stay – for three months – fishing and snoozing, and living on the sweet pure scent of pine, and of bacon sizzling on a cast iron skillet over a crackling fire. It was a y'all come camp – friends, family, any one with a fishing pole and a sleeping bag was welcome.

You can probably tell from the job descriptions, he was not a rich man. He had built his modestly furnished three-bedroom, one bath bungalow in Hollywood in around 1915, and lived there the rest of his life.

How did he pull off Easy Street with so little money in his pocket?

Low expectations.

They ate at home. All their services were within walking distance. His idea of entertainment was reading the *Hollywood Citizen* newspaper, or listening to wrestling matches on the radio and later on a tiny black and white TV. No European vacation dreams. No Pinterest-produced visions of over-the-top dinner parties. No fancy cars. No elegant wardrobe.

Simple. And simply wonderful.

To be fair, perhaps one of the reasons there were no European vacation dreams was because Grandad had circled the globe twice by the time he was fourteen. Perhaps it's much easier to stay put when you've crammed a whole lifetime into your first quarter century.

While still in his teens, Grandad made his way to the Southwest, likely El Paso, Texas. There he worked for the Mounted Guard, the precursor to the Border Patrol. His favorite Mounted Guard story involved a shootout. In the middle of the fray, he looked down at his boot, thinking he had stepped in a puddle. It was a puddle, all right – of his own blood. He had been shot in the foot.

Grandad finally joined his father and brother in Hollywood

in 1891. When my mother asked him as a child how he got there, his answer was, "Why on horseback, you silly!"

It is likely he went to work for his father building bungalows fairly early on. We know that he also worked at the Alligator Farm, a tourist attraction, and an ostrich farm in Pasadena. Ostrich-plumed ladies hats were very popular at the time.

Grandad also found plenty of opportunity to use his horseback riding skills. For years, as a side job, he broke horses in Beachwood Canyon in the Hollywood Hills, earning him the nickname Bronco Bill.

One of his most significant jobs was stationary steam engineer for the Fremont Hotel in downtown Los Angeles. That meant he operated the machinery that provided steam energy to the hotel. The reason the job was significant was because the hotel placed him right in the path of his soon-to-be-wife, Bam. She and her sister had moved to Los Angeles from Wisconsin and were working as waitresses at a restaurant near the Fremont. As Grandad told it, "When she walked down the street, she had the cutest wiggle I ever saw." They were married for fifty-seven years.

Tinkerer. Family man. Adventurer. World-class storyteller.

Such a character was he that those who knew him don't need to consult scrapbooks. He is well preserved within our hearts and minds.

Lincoln (1876-1978) Paternal great-grandfather

Talk about a promoter... In all his 102 years, his mind never stopped. Due to his longevity, much of what we know about him came right from the source. The rest is documented in the ephemera he left behind – letters; theatre programs; newspaper articles by and about him; books; plaques; photographs.

As explained in a letter he wrote to my grandmother in 1973, when he was ninety-eight years old, Lincoln was destined to be a showman from the start. It reads:

To Imo - some notes

All the world's a stage – the people are the players.

While I was not known as an actor, I did many parts and was an entertainer at clubs around New York. Living in New

York I had the opportunity to see the best big shows. I became attached to the theatre while I had my first job as an insurance clerk. I usually "took in" a Saturday matinee and the Grand Operas. We had two pianos and a small organ in our big house. Music was a family tradition. As a boy I sang in the famous Trinity Church Choir.

Vaudeville shows took my fancy and I used to imitate the performers song and dance in our kitchen at home – our Irish cook was my audience.

I became a song and dance man. Beginning my professional career with Red Irwin & Irwin & Hart, we played the vaudeville circuit on the East Coast, etc.

When I wrote my brother Franklin I was marrying an actress, he wired me in Portland, "Don't marry an actress."

How wrong can people be?

Father

Lincoln went West first in 1900. There is a production photo of him with two other actors taken in Pershing Square in Los Angeles in 1903.

My father's favorite story from this period of Lincoln's life was about a time he arrived in the Old Union Station in downtown L.A. to find hawkers with buggies awaiting the passengers. What they were hawking was land. The offer was lunch and a tour of the new Wilshire District. With time on his hands, Abraham took them up on it. The agents extolled the opportunity to own a lot on Wilshire Boulevard. For fifty dollars! Lincoln said, he thought to himself, *I'm too smart to fall for that!* Several years later, driving down bustling Wilshire Boulevard, he chuckled to himself, *Well, that was a damn stupid mistake!*

After several years in Oregon and Ohio, working in theatre and advertising, Abraham received an offer from Thomas Ince to move to Culver City, California and work as a production manager in his movie studio. Thus began the story of the family's journey west – a story so captivating that hearing it never gets old.

Rather than take the train, Abraham decided to pack his wife and sons into their 1917 Buick ragtop touring car, along with a few necessities, and venture across the country on the Lincoln Highway, which was established in 1913.

My grandfather told me that in the sparser areas of the west, cars would get to a station, then wait for other cars to join up with them, so they weren't travelling alone. That turned out to be the family's salvation on the detour that almost led to their deaths.

This is a grand prize winner of a story, which the grandkids never tired of hearing. The following narration by Lincoln is taken from an article that appeared in the *Salt Lake City Herald* dated July 6, 1919. Headline: FAMILY NEAR DEATH OF THIRST IN DESERT.

"We left Orr's Ranch early on the morning of July 4, and attempted to take a shortcut to Fish Springs to the new highway which is now practically finished. Another party followed closely in their automobile. Before noon we learned we had taken a wrong road, and soon after found our cars running in deep sand. Our water supply was so low that it was impossible to continue, as our motors were burning up. It was then decided that the other party should return to Orr's Ranch for water and information, while we were to await their return.

"We waited until nightfall for his return, but he did not come. We were weak from lack of water, and our throats were dry and parched. The children suffered terribly. Something had to be done quickly, so we decided to walk in an endeavor to find water rather than die from thirst without an attempt. I carried the smallest child and we started to drag ourselves through the heavy sand.

"At last we found we could go no farther. We sank down in the hot sand and panted for breath, and slowly lapsed into unconsciousness. The last words I remember were from one of the children, who asked, 'Papa, are we going to die?' I was too weak to answer.

"In the meantime the tourist had reached the ranch, and after hurriedly placing water aboard, started back for us with Mr. Orr. Of course, under Mr. Orr's direction, he took the right road back to our machine and did not find us there... We found later that they had discovered the track in the sand of one of the children's' sandals, and knew we had left our car and attempted to walk. They followed these tracks by throwing the rays of the automobile searchlight on the sand and occasionally getting out and examining the roadway.

"It was midnight, they told us later, when they discovered us lying prone upon the sand. We were all unconscious, they said, but Mrs. Hart recovered enough after a few minutes to whisper. With plentiful applications of water we all regained consciousness soon and gave thanks that we were no worse than badly weakened from our experience. Mr. Orr took us to his ranch, where everything possible was done for our comfort.

"Our experience has not made us abandon our trip west, but it has certainly taught us a severe lesson in following roads, especially across the desert. Hereafter, we will be glad to stay on the road marked Lincoln Highway, and our narrow escape from a terrible death should be a warning to other tourists not to attempt shortcuts."

In my grandfather's version of the story, he said that he wasn't completely unconscious, but that he was seeing mirages. So, when he began to see lights bob slowly up and down and move toward him, he thought it was one of the mirages. It was, however, their rescuers. He also vividly remembers the Mr. Orrs for their being Mormon and having very long beards.

Abraham's entry on the Lincoln Highway Guide's memoranda page, simply states, "Got lost in the desert and were rescued at 11 o'clock. Got supper and retired at midnight of the 4th. Stayed all night and all day the 5th. 5 meals - beds - 1 loaf of bread - $26. Left on the 6th for Fish Springs."

Talk about a man who didn't let things faze him!

We are fortunate to have the story of the family's years in Culver City in Lincoln's own words. They are taken from a speech he made to the Culver City Rotary Club, November 1949, when he was seventy-five years old. This is a small portion of the speech:

"I remember when I first came to Los Angeles in 1900, I saw a big sign-board erected by William M. Garland, the realtor, which read 'Los Angeles Population 200,000 by 1910.' Having come out here from the conservative East, I put Garland's advertising down as an overstatement of optimism. We know now that his prediction was really an understatement.

"One day there appeared a young enterprising feller by the name of Harry Culver, who is said to have told a friend that he had acquired a piece of land which he planned to cut up into town lots. The friend, after hearing of its location, expressed an opinion that as a town site it was zero.

"As the plot thickens, Culver, in his big black Cadillac and his cream colored chamois gloves, drove up the coast to a little motion picture village called 'Inceville,' just north of Santa Monica. Here he met another enterprising feller by the name of Thomas H. Ince.

"Culver induced Ince and his associates to move his picture making to his town site by giving him twenty acres of land upon which to build a modern motion picture studio. Culver figured that he needed industry and a payroll to sell his town lots. The Triangle Picture Company was quickly built on the twenty acres, with Ince and his associates, Mack Sennett and David W. Griffith making the Triangle.

"However, after a short period Griffith and Hart moved to other lots, and Ince sold the new studio and the twenty acres to Sam Goldwyn and associates from New York – and it became Goldwyn Studios.

"Now, Tom Ince made a good deal and found himself making more money at selling studios than he made in selling pictures. So, with a pocket full of folding money, he struck out for himself as an independent producer, while Harry Culver's town lots were now really moving and his pockets began to bulge also.

"After the Goldwyn people moved in, back went Ince to Culver and got another twenty acres on the same terms as his first. Here Ince built perhaps the most up-to-date studio at that time, with every facility for picture making, with an imposing administration building facing the main thoroughfare, Washington Boulevard – a dusty road at the time.

"Things began to move, and Culver City developed, with fewer lima beans and jackrabbits. With the advent of the picture industry, homes went up, new streets and improvements went in, and a town was born.

"Culver City could have been the Motion Picture Capital of the World, but in Hollywood they had a Chamber of Commerce that stole the show by proclaiming Hollywood Boulevard the Glamour Promenade, where actors gathered at street corners to be seen by tourists and tell lies about big salaries. They wore their makeup, sans dark glasses. They didn't try to hide their identity in those early days.

"Culver City's movie stars were just like other people. They were neighbors. While most of the men folk in the community worked in the studios, housewives and children played bit parts and extras, with nice paychecks to be spent with the local merchants, whose stores were crude, but friendly. The town was devoid of sin, sex, shame, and sordidness. In fact, you could say that, generally, things were considered pretty dull.

"Ince's arrival in Culver City was followed by other young fellers with plenty of ambition and little money. Henry Lehrman built a fresh air stage where comedies were made, using our streets and stores for sets. Hal Roach arrived with one camera and some scripts for *Our Gang Comedies*. Warner Brothers took over a small adobe building used by boy scouts.

"One personality whose job in Culver City brought joy and laughter to everyone was Will Rogers. He was making pictures at Goldwyn's. At ten o'clock one morning, the people supporting him were on the set ready with cameras set and everything ready except the star. Will was late as usual. Where was he? Holding up production, at the rate of about a thousand dollars an hour, all hands standing around waiting. His home was contacted. He had been gone for some time. Finally, he was located in a vacant lot in back of the school house, showing a bunch of kids how to twirl a rope. Will used to ride an old horse from the studio, down Washington Boulevard to a little restaurant on the corner, where he'd tie up his horse and eat lunch with the gang. He was the most natural man I ever met.

"My old friends Tom Ince and Harry Culver are gone. These men laid the foundations of the motion picture industry. As I passed my old studio, I tipped my hat in salute to the fine people who work with me, and the fine people who lived here, and helped put Culver City on the map."

We celebrated Lincoln's 100th birthday in 1976 at the El Cortez Hotel in San Diego. My father was standing in the back with a couple of writers from the military press, waiting for Abraham to make his appearance. He could tell they thought this was just going to be another instance of an old guy being wheeled out to be feted by family. And then Lincoln walked up onto the stage, his back ramrod straight, and took the microphone. The first words out of his mouth were, "If someone will bring me a scotch, we'll get this thing started." And then he proceeded to regale us with story after story of one helluva life!

He and his wife are buried in Fort Rosecrans National Cemetery in Point Loma.

Raymond (1905-1960) Maternal grandfather

I include this story as an example of one so dramatic that as a child I asked to hear it over and over.

It took place in 1934, when Ray was on a sales trip to Arizona. He was driving on a twisty road just outside of Kingman. It was after dark. He came around a curve too fast and swerved, but couldn't correct his trajectory. The car plummeted down a 100 foot cliff. On impact, Ray was thrown onto a railroad track. Hearing the crash, nuns from a nearby convent rushed to the scene. There they found Ray unconscious – with a train fast approaching. They waved the skirts of their habits, stopping the train. Someone came with a car, and Ray was pronounced dead at the scene. When they got to the hospital in Kingman, a doctor found a pulse.

Ray had broken every bone in his body, but he was alive! They wrapped him in a full body cast. His hospital recovery lasted for a few weeks.

My mother recalls the train ride with her brother and mother to pick him up and return him home. The trip was so memorable an experience, even though she was quite young, the details are vivid in her mind. Before they got there, her train collided with a semi-truck carrying grapes. She remembers getting off and picking up grapes from the track.

In order to get Ray into the train for his ride back to Hollywood, they had to slide him on a stretcher through the window. He was in that cast so long, my mother remembers him sticking a yardstick down it to scratch his back. When the cast finally came off, he walked with a limp – one that stayed with him for the rest of his life. He also had to have experienced pain and arthritis, but he didn't complain. In fact, his very first job after a year of recuperation was with the Post Office, where he had to lift heavy packages. But it was the Depression, and you took whatever work you could find. Under the circumstances, the family moved in with Bam and

Grandad. And they stayed for fifteen years.

I was only seven when my grandfather died. I had called him Bobby, for whatever reason my young mind dubbed him that. A sweet, sweet man, he had been my favorite person on earth. He would take me on his rounds while collecting the rent at my uncle's hotels. Laurel Canyon was our connector between the Valley and Hollywood. We were on it a lot, as they were back living in Hollywood, and we had moved to Pacoima and then on to North Hollywood with thousands of other young families. I can still feel every curve of that road. I also can see him in our kitchen, stopping by to have lunch with me, my siblings, and my mother. My Bobby had very large hands. They made me feel safe. He made me feel treasured. The greatest gift you can give a child. Why *do* the good die young?

Dad & Mom

I concluded this chapter with a long and detailed account of my parents' childhoods in Southern California. I was fortunate enough to be able to get the stories right from them.

Again, lives don't have to have been extraordinary. The ordinary becomes fascinating when it's your own flesh and blood. Your stories are a gift you're giving to future generations. So, talk to your elders. Ask: Who were their friends? What was their house like? Their neighborhood? What were their favorite pets? First jobs? Favorite singers? Favorite movies? Did they have any encounters with famous people? How did they wear their hair? How did they dress? What was their favorite dessert? What sports did they play? Did they dance? What kinds of celebrations did they share with friends and family? Where did they vacation? What hobbies did they enjoy?

As I said at the beginning of the chapter, for my parents it was, indeed, a wonderful life.

Bam and Grandad's Hollywood bungalow continued to be a draw for family, extended family, and friends well into my childhood.

That and the star-strewn boulevards of the Hollywood of the 1880s to the 1960s are every bit as alive now as they were then.

It has been my privilege to stroll them once again, through...

The magic of memory.

The magic of stories.

Epilogue

Our family does not tend to hold your average funeral. Rather, we do unique memorials and event burials. Though to outsiders they may appear odd and perhaps even a tad irreverent, I believe they define the magnificent soul of our family, both now and long past.

And so I end with the Globe Theatre Rose Garden story...

Several months after the passing of my great-aunt Irene my cousin was talking to my father on the phone. During the course of the conversation, my cousin mentioned that he wasn't sure what to do with his mother's ashes.

Light bulb moment! "I know exactly what to do with them," my father said. "We'll spread them in the rose garden at the Globe Theatre in Balboa Park. Her portrayals of Shakespeare's famous female characters at both the Old Globe in San Diego and at the Chicago World's Fair embody her acting career."

My cousin thought it was a great idea.

Soon, the two hopped a plane to San Diego and proceeded to the park.

All was quiet outside the Globe when they arrived. After checking to see that the surrounding area was empty of visitors, they stepped gingerly into the rose bed.

Gently opening the urn, they began spreading the ashes around the plants. Halfway through their endeavor, every door to the Globe swung open, and out poured the theatre-goers. It was intermission!

Caught in the act, they casually finished the job and stepped out of the garden bed, like they were official rose inspectors. "No aphids here," said the expression on their faces, and off they strolled. Mission accomplished!

When you embrace the quirky; when you find the extraordinary in the ordinary; when you share the deepest grief and the greatest joy with those you love; when you step into that which you fear:

A voyage in steerage to an unfamiliar land...

A military transport to a war zone...

A train to yet another city and another sales call...

A corral containing an unbroken stallion...

The birth of a child...

The death of a child...

A reprimand by your community...

A speech...

A confrontation...

An exhibit of your art...

Opening night...

There you stand – vulnerable and exposed. And there you've done it! You've lived! You've really, really lived!

I had a lot of fun writing the "Royalty" chapter. I love to imagine that I have a little Herleva coursing through my veins.

But it is the common folk that this book is truly about. Common folk who lived uncommon lives. They are the threads that wove a nation. A nation! I couldn't be more proud of them. Yes, that means you too, Charles.

9

END MATTER

WHERE THE BODIES ARE BURIED

This is the first section of end matter that I included in my book. It is an A to Z ancestor list, indicating the websites on which I found information on these ancestors. I included it for relatives who might want to do further research on their own. Not all ancestors whose stories are in the book are on the websites, so they are not included on this list.

For ancestors like Christopher Branch, who is included on the ancestor list, there is an abundant amount of material which I haven't covered. Be aware that facts often conflict between the websites.

I often only list one family member on this record, as additional family members may be found through links on the same website page.

If you are like me and like to include visits to dead people while traveling, be warned that even with the location of the grave in hand, markers are often hard to spot. And many cemeteries don't have offices, or they have limited office hours. We have been known to wander for hours without finding our ancestors. We finally achieved success on a second trip to the Beeler graves in Pittsburgh, when we flagged down the caretaker and he spotted their markers almost completely covered in grass.

Information and websites in this section are listed as follows:
Name; Birth Year (in parentheses) (not always accurate)**;
Family Tree Number; Location of Grave;**
Wikitree **(*Wt);** *Wikipedia* **(*Wp); and** *Find a Grave* **(*F)**
*The abbreviations indicate on which websites the ancestor may be found. There is often a short bio on the *Wikitree* and *Find a Grave* pages. Please note that the word *buried* on a listing indicates that only the city or town where the ancestor is buried is known. The location of the grave itself and/or cemetery is unknown.

For illustrative purposes, here is an excerpt of my ancestor list...
Barnes, Joshua (1615)–114 – **Wt** – & wife Sarah Jackson – Buried Rye, NY
Bassett, Alan (1158)–176 – **Wt**
David Beeler (1793)–210– Allegheny Cemetery, Pittsburgh – **F**
Beyeler, Jacob (1687)–218 – Amish–Mennonite Cemetery, Morgantown, PA – **Wt**
Bissell, John, Captain (1591)– 367 – Palisado Cemetery, Windsor, CT – **Wt & F**
Bradt, Albert (1607)–274 & *Andries* (1578)–276 – Buried in Rensselaerswyck, Albany, NY
Branch, Christopher (1602)–290 – Kingsland Plantation, Branch Family Cemetery, Henrico Co., VA – **Wt, Wp & F**
Channel, Jeremiah (1754)–280 – Buried near Bowling Green Church, Licking Co., OH; 1/4 m. N, 1/4 m. W, along PA RR on hill in field, second row of graves in corner of field, N side of SR 585; 1909 stone then standing now broken and could only find footstone and part of headstone – **Wt**
Currence, William (1727)–263 – Mill Creek, Randolph Co., WV – **Wt & F**
de Ferrers, Robert (1068)–184 – **Wt**
deHooges, Johannes (1588)–278 – Buried Beverwyck, NY
Deyo, Reverend Julia Amanda Halstead (1838)–88 – Highland Cemetery, Ulster Co., NY; Sec. C, Lot 162-164 – **Wp & F**

WHERE THEY LIVED

This is the second section of end matter. It is a list of addresses that I found for some of my ancestors. I thought it would be fun to include them, in the event that my relatives wanted take a peak at the residences if they were in the vicinity. In some cases the original homes are no longer standing. I thought relatives still might enjoy discovering a lingering ancient palm or oak that witnessed the comings and goings of our family. For the purposes of this book, I have included two sample addresses only. The entries include the ancestors' birth dates in parentheses and Family Tree Chart numbers.

California
John Doe (1916) – 156
123 Main Street
Hollywood, CA

England
Jane Doe (1725) – 154
Reedly Hall
Hampstead Heath

PHOTOGRAPHS

To simplify the printing process I placed photographs at the very end of my family history book. I used single-sided gloss 80# stock paper for the photographs – 20# double-sided for the rest of the book.
Also to simplify the process and to save paper, I didn't attempt to put captions under each photograph. Instead, I preceded the Photograph pages with Caption pages, as follows:

I divided the photos into family groups that I used as a heading at the top of the Caption Pages:

Smith – Jones – Anderson – Morgan Family Photo Captions

Under the heading, I included the following information for each section:

Photo captions are organized by Page Number; Photos Left to Right, Row by Row; and People within Photo Groups Left to Right. The first time I include a name, I use the full name. After that, if it is clear who the person is, I only use the first name.

The photograph pages are numbered, starting with the number one, completely separate from the pagination for the rest of the book.
I listed the photo captions according to the photo page number, as follows:

Page 1
Photo 1: Standing, back row: Mary Smith, John Smith, Elizabeth Jones. Standing, front row: Darby Anderson, Dale Anderson, Jr. Seated: Jim Bell, Sr. & Jane Bell. Photo taken at Jane's home in Beverly Hills.
Photo 2: Darby
Photo 3: Darby, Dale & John

FORMATTING AND PUBLISHING YOUR FAMILY HISTORY

There are several different ways to go with this.

The most simple way is to use the print and copy services at a company like Fed Ex Office or Staples. FedEx Office has a Family History/Presentations printing option already set up. With it, you can "tell your story with a presentation booklet that features family photos, stories and more. Orders include binding, front and back covers, and tabs." If you choose Staples, you will find what you're looking for in the Presentations and Manual options. The people working at these businesses are generally more than happy to help you with your project.

If you'd like to create a paperback version of your family history, there are a couple ways to go. Brick and mortar printing businesses willing to produce small numbers of books are rare, but I was able to find one in my area. It can get quite expensive if you are only printing a handful of books. An order of 50 cost me about $20 each. An order of 10 was $32 each. They may offer book cover design for a price. Or, you can create your own. You will need to talk with them about the best way to proceed. To save money, everything except my cover was printed in black and white, including the photographs.

Another option for creating a paperback version of your family history is to do it through an online publishing company like: Book Baby, Blurb, or Lulu. These companies vary in cost, time to publish, shipping times, print quality, cover quality, and services like cover creation. It's best to explore their websites to find what best suits your needs. And definitely look for reviews from people who have used their services.

FAMILY TREE SAMPLE

The following is the introduction I included with my Family Tree Charts:

Had I created a family tree with all the branches it would have been huge! What you will find on the following pages are charts that *do not* include my entire family. They instead include ancestors whose stories are in the book, signified by the bolded names. On the charts, I include spouses whose stories are not in the book in non-bolded font for information purposes. *The numbers in front of ancestors' names are exclusive to that ancestor.*

The family group names are at the top of each page, next to the chart number. The further back the generations go, the less exact the birth and death dates. The range can be as much as five to fifteen years. I often use *c.* for *circa* if I don't know the date. *m.* means *married.*

Note for the purposes of the sample tree chart that follows, I used the ancestor's relation to me in place of a first name. I only include **collateral relatives** *whose stories are in my family history book. According to Family Tree Magazine: "A collateral relative is any blood relative who is* **not** *your* **direct ancestor**. *So your* **ancestors** *are your parents, grandparents, great-grandparents, etc., and your* **collateral relatives** *are cousins, nieces, nephews, aunts, uncles, siblings, etc."*

In my book, Charts 1 through 5 consist of my mother's side of the family. Charts 6 through 9 are my father's side. The number of charts in your book will depend entirely on how many ancestors you include.

Chart 1 – Smith; Olsen; Hardy; Able

Generation 1
1–Mother Smith (1932) m. **2–Father Jones(1932)**
　　　***3–Uncle Smith (1930-1983)** – Mother's Brother
　　　***4–Aunt Smith (1940-2016)** – Mother's Sister
Uncle Smith & Aunt Smith are examples of collateral relatives whose stories are in my book. Thus the reason for their inclusion on the family tree.
Generation 2
5–Grandfather Smith (1905–1960)
　　　　m. **6–Grandmother Olsen (1906–1970)**
Generation 3
7–Great-grandfather Smith (1877-1955)
　　　m. **8–Great-grandmother Hardy (1875–1933)**
Generation 4
9–Great-great-grandfather Smith (1838-1901)
　　　m. 10–Great-great-grandmother Able (1837-1911)
　　　***11–3rd-great-Uncle Able (1835-1862**)
　　　　　– Great-great-grandmother Able's brother
Uncle Able is another collateral relative whose story is in the book. Thus the reason for his inclusion on the family tree. Note that Great-great-grandmother Able's name is not in bold, because there is no story about her in the book.

To Where the Sun Sets

10

RESOURCES

Within this section, I list websites that will help you research and publish your family history. I included a resource section in my family history book in the event any of my relatives wanted to research on their own.

This is not intended as an endorsement of any of the listed companies/businesses/websites.

PRIMARY SOURCES

Connect. Connect. Connect. Please.

Yes. I wrote this book because I love history and I love my family – which after this exercise has grown exponentially.

But I also wrote it to inspire you to research and record your own stories. I want you to connect with your past – first, by connecting with your present. That means any friend or relative who has a story from which you can build your history. Your aunt, step-brother, life-long family friend, cousin who you're not really sure is a cousin. Talk to them. Dig up old letters and photographs. Visit places that are of significance to your family.

If you like to write, I encourage you to take your research, interviews, letters, diaries, and photographs, and compile them into a book. Use this one as a model, if you like. I chose to organize mine into thematic chapters because my focus is stories. You might prefer a chronological approach rather than themes, using the family trees as your guide. One note on interviews: use your smartphone or a digital recorder, and take notes as well. Also, if typing is not your favorite thing, there are any number of *speech/voice to text* options you can find on the internet. Just google *speech to text* and choose the one that best suits your computer or device.

If you're overwhelmed by the thought of *writing* a family history, there is a fine alternative – *record* an oral history in video. In the mid-1970s, when no one even owned a video recorder, my father rented one from a camera shop and invited my grandparents over. They brought old family photographs; spread them out on a picnic bench in our backyard; took a seat; my father focused the video camera on them; and for the next hour, one by one, they held the photos up to the recorder and told about the people and the stories behind them. To our family, that video is priceless.

You don't need fancy video equipment anymore. Good inexpensive cameras have video capability. And there's always that smartphone sitting in your pocket.

You can't create a family history in a vacuum – or within a glass box. You need living, breathing people to help you. And when you connect with them, you're taking a stand for two-sided, face-to-face conversation – an absolute necessity for peace on our planet, and to help each other understand that we are part of a whole and we matter to it. Every one of us.

SECONDARY SOURCES

PEDIGREE CHARTS & FAMILY GROUP SHEETS

Whether a book or oral history, you need *Pedigree Charts* and *Family Group Sheets* to anchor your work. A Pedigree Chart is just a fancy name for Family Tree. Family Group Sheets contain information on one individual family. You can find templates of these by entering the search terms: *Pedigree Chart forms, Family Tree forms,* and *Family Group Sheet forms.* Check them out, and choose them to fit your needs. There's quite a variety of them: from simple forms to large fancy family trees fit for hanging on your wall. Some are free. Some a few dollars.

I prefer the simple ones that you fill in yourself. It involves a lot of writing, but it's also a way to imprint your ancestors' lives in your mind. I usually write in pencil, because these are working documents that I edit as I discover additional information on my ancestors.

My personal favorites are the free ones from the National Archives website: *archives.gov/research/genealogy/charts-forms.* The Family Group Sheet form has two pages. The second page is a place to list information on all the children.

GENEALOGY WEBSITES

You're probably not going to get very far by using information gleaned only from your family members for your family tree charts and group sheets, and for researching and writing your stories. You're going to need genealogy websites. I avoid websites that offer information for free in exchange for my contact information, unless I have thoroughly vetted the company. I'm one of those people who approaches the internet with a high degree of wariness, using incognito browsing whenever I can.

If you enter the search term **genealogy websites** *you're going to find a bucket load of websites to help you with your research. Some, like* familyhistorydaily.com *and* ngsgenealogy.org (National Genealogical Society)*, offer lists of what they consider to be the best of the genealogy sites. Others are the genealogy websites themselves. Below is my list of genealogy websites, starting with the ones I use the most frequently, followed by others I thought you might find helpful in alphabetical order.*

WikiTree.com – The site I use the most.

From their website: *Our mission is to grow an accurate single family tree that connects us all and is freely available to us all.*

One of the best things about it is the links both forward and backward in an ancestral line. The information provided comes from an endless number of sources, including books, articles, Ancestry.com, research projects, family histories, etc. A source list appears at the bottom of many of the entries. Like Wikipedia, there are times the information is inaccurate, but I often found the sources to be impressive and reliable. Pay attention to them; you can use them for further research on other relatives.

When I search a name on Wikitree, I choose to sort the names by *birthdate*, and then use the birthdate to identify the ancestor. If you don't do that, you may find yourself searching through 1500+ Robert Williams.

Note that names are often spelled any number of ways. In Wikitree, Johann Leonhart Ziegler is spelled Johann *Leonhardt Zeigler*.

Wikipedia.com

I use it all the time, and find it very helpful. Although, for genealogy research my only ancestors to be found there are ones who achieved some degree of fame or historical significance.

Findagrave.com

I also use this site a lot. I appreciate that they often include a short bio on the interred and that they include links to other ancestors. From Wikipedia: "Find a Grave is an American website that allows the public to search and add to an online database of cemetery records. It is owned by Ancestry.com. It receives and uploads digital photographs of headstones from burial sites, taken by unpaid volunteers at cemeteries. Find a Grave then posts the photo on its website."

Ancestry.com

If you want to make your life easy and don't mind spending the money, this is the way to go. They've got everything you need to do your ancestry research right at your fingertips. In the 90s, I decided to join for a year to research my husband's family. I squeezed a lot into that time. Ancestry has varying subscriptions. The basic is the DNA, which gives you your DNA breakdown by country/region and some information on your ancestors' immigration patterns. After that, you can pay for access to United States records of all kinds, and for even more money, access to world records. I'm not including cost, because it varies with the plan you want and is subject to change. I do know they have sales every few months.

23andme.com

This is a health and ancestry DNA website with which most people are familiar. I used it for both. I enjoyed seeing the breakdown of my ancestry, and was relieved to discover I am a low risk for whateveropesia. One of this company's main goals is DNA/medical research, therefore unless you opt out of email solicitations to participate in research studies, you will receive many requests to do so. After completing a couple of the surveys, I lost interest because of the length of time it took to complete them. It may also be because if I filled out every survey request I receive from all quarters, I could make it a career. Watch for sales if you're interested in giving them your spit.

Books.google.com

This is really cool if you have never used it. For instance, when I was looking for something on the Gilmorettes, the singing group my aunt was in, a Google search of the name led me to an article in *Billboard Magazine* from November 28, 1942. The search term is even highlighted in the document, making it easier for you to find. The copies can be blurry. From the website:

Book Search works just like web search. When we find a book with content that contains a match for your search terms, we'll link to it in your search results.

If the book is out of copyright, or the publisher has given us permission, you'll be able to see a preview of the book, and in some cases the entire text. If it's in the public domain, you're free to download a PDF copy.

We've created reference pages for every book so you can quickly find all kinds of relevant information: book reviews, web references, maps and more.

If you find a book you like, click on the "Buy this book" and "Borrow this book" links to see where you can buy or borrow the print book.

Castlegarden.org

"A free database developed and funded by The Battery Conservancy. It contains and makes available eleven million records of immigrants who arrived at the Port of New York from 1820 - 1892."

Familysearch.org

The world's largest collection of free genealogy records.

Go.newspapers.com

This is an Ancestry company.

"The largest online newspaper archive."

This is one I'd be tempted to fork over the money and join. I love newspapers – old ones, anyway. And they have obituaries, articles, and photos from over 16,000 of them and counting.

Home.rootsweb.com

"The Internet's oldest and largest *free* genealogical community." Requires an account.

Moravianchurcharchives.org

The Moravian Archives is the official repository for the records of the Moravian Church in America – Northern Province. The Northern Province covers the Moravian churches in the United States (excluding congregations located in North Carolina, Florida, Georgia and Virginia) and Canada.

Moravianarchives.net

With archival facilities around the world, the employees collect and preserve the records of the Moravian Church and make them available to the public. This site serves as a central hub to guide patrons in locating, contacting, and visiting the facilities that hold records pertinent to their research.

National Archives – archives.gov

You can imagine how many records our government holds in its archives. Be sure to use this tool to help in your ancestry research.

Military Records – archives.gov/research/military

The National Archives holds Federal military service records from the Revolutionary War to 1912 in the National Archives Building in Washington, D.C.

Census Data –
archives.gov/research/genealogy/census/about

Census data takes some digging. If you decide to buy an Ancestry.com subscription, you can find most of the census information you're looking for through that. Otherwise, the National Archives has a very thorough explanation of where the records can be found on the website address listed above. Note that you have to follow links to Census Resources, and one of those, naturally, is Ancestry.com.

From the website: "The National Archives has the census schedules on microfilm available from 1790 to 1940, and online access is available through our digitization partners (free at any National Archives facility). See our Census Resources page to search the digitized records on our partners' websites. (Please note: Most of the 1890 Census was destroyed in a Department of Commerce fire in 1921, though partial records are available for some states.)"

Quaker Meeting Records – swarthmore.edu/friends-
historical-library/quaker-meeting-records

Friends Historical Library (FHL) is an official depository for the records of many North American yearly meetings of the Society of Friends. Its holdings include over 3700 linear feet of original archives: membership books, minutes, and other original records. FHL also holds over 2500 reels of microfilm of Friends' records from Canada, United States, Britain, and Ireland.

Statue of Liberty – Ellis Island Foundation –
libertyellis.org

Ship and passenger lists, immigration records

Usgenweb.org – The USGenWeb Project

From the website: "Founded by genealogists, the idea was to provide a single entry point for genealogy data and research. Although The USGenWeb Project was originally designed to be organized by state and county, much genealogy data cannot be limited to a single county, or even a single state. So, USGenWeb Special Projects have evolved to collect and disseminate data that goes beyond county and state lines."

Veterans' Gravesite Locators:
The American Battle Monuments Commission – abmc.gov

The American Battle Monuments Commission provides information on service members buried in overseas cemeteries.

Arlington National Cemetery – arlingtoncemetery.mil/Explore/Find-a-Grave

The Arlington National Cemetery provides information on service members buried there.

US Department of Veterans Affairs – gravelocator.cem.va.gov

From the website: "Search for burial locations of veterans and their family members in VA National Cemeteries, state veterans cemeteries, various other military and Department of Interior cemeteries, and for veterans buried in private cemeteries when the grave is marked with a government grave marker.

"The Nationwide Gravesite Locator includes burial records from many sources. These sources provide varied data; some searches may contain less information than others. Information on veterans buried in private cemeteries was collected for the purpose of furnishing government grave markers, and we do not have information available for burials prior to 1997."

Worldgenweb.org

The WorldGenWeb Project is a non-profit, volunteer-based organization dedicated to providing genealogical and historical records and resources for world-wide access.

To Where the Sun Sets

ABOUT THE AUTHOR

A fifth-generation Californian, Susan Hart Snyder lives with her husband in California's gold country in the home in which they raised their two sons. She ended up on the edge of the Central Valley in the foothills of the Sierras after spending her youth in two very different valleys – San Fernando and Silicon.

Susan has a B.A. in English and an M.A. in Creative Writing.

She has published personal and motivational essays, feature, and travel articles. She has also written and published a novel series – the *Sydney Roberts Series*; and an essay collection – *Living the Little Things*.

Get more advice on researching and writing your family history, and read more about her other stories on her website: susanhartsnyder.com.

Printed in Great Britain
by Amazon

83944688R00072